YOUR

The businesswoman's companion for a
sparkling personal brand

Lily Naadu Mensah

Paperback ISBN 978-0-9955625-0-9

Kindle ISBN 978-0-9955625-1-6

Published in the UK by Lyncs Press

www.lyncspress.com

DEDICATION

All my gratitude goes to the Divine whose unwavering favour guides my every step. I dedicate this to my all-time shero, my mum Theodora Engmann whose hand and gentle guidance has been immeasurable in the woman I am today. To my big Sister 'Sta' Abigail Tagoe Nee Parkes – the clips round the ears she dutifully gave me as a gobby teen, so I would straighten up and fly right. To my three heartbeats, my children Kenneth Otoo-Quayson, Theodora Otoo-Quayson and Samuel Yeboah – all of whom have taught me patience, tenacity, selfless love, and the need to create a legacy. You are my inspiration. Thank you.

To my grandmothers, Helena 'Mother' Azu and Anna 'Maa' Allotey, who didn't live to see this publication but whose entrepreneurial spirit lives within me. Few baked cakes and ran con-current government contracts like Mother in Osu; and if you said, you could buy better Kenkey compared to Maa's all the way from Prampram to Asylum Down, you will be labelled as spreading fake news! They were both powerhouses in their fields and I'm so grateful for their legacies.

EARLY REVIEWS

"This book is a must read if you're unsure about what 'Branding' is or unclear about how you define and create a personal brand. It's essential for anyone embarking on an entrepreneurial journey, or wanting to establish themselves as a brand. Lily has managed to create a book which is easy to read, practical and informative.

No matter what stage of the journey you're on, Work your Quirks will have something for you. Despite my years as a Public Relations' professional, I too will definitely be taking a leaf out of this book. It reminds me, we continue to learn on a daily basis and can never stop developing and growing."

Evadney Campbell MBE
Former BBC Journalist, now Co-founder, Shiloh PR

"Work Your Quirks, is exactly what it says. Lily's approach to having a dazzling brand is rich with lots of meaty content thrown in with some light humour. It portrays a mixed blend of simple tips and strategies to encourage any business owner to start reviewing how their brand represents them.

Her book is direct and concise and gets you thinking instantly about how you can start implementing some of the strategies highlighted. I highly recommend it. It's the sort of book you can draw reference from, for that all important meeting, speaking event or networking opportunity.

An Inspiring and fresh approach to personal branding. I loved it!"
Victoria Awele Griffith
Founder & CEO, Spectacular Woman CIC

"This book is written in a very simple way and in small workable chunks, easy to digest and to put into practice straight away. I especially loved links to other resources, tables and worksheets – I found them extremely useful. They turn the book into a workbook so I can practise

as I read. The book is full of tips and real life examples. "Work Your QUIRKs" is the A to Z for any woman who runs her own business. Recommended!!"

Lina Bourdon
MD, City & Country Financial Services Ltd

"Work your Quirks is the most comprehensive book that I have come across on developing your personal brand. Using the inspired metaphor of the diamond, Lily Mensah demystifies how to define your unique brand, what to wear and even how to network effortlessly.

This book is perfect for those who want to reinvent themselves, perhaps after stepping out of corporate life and those who want to finally take charge of how they are seen rather than leaving it to chance. The process of reinvention and developing your authentic brand will go more smoothly once you have the knowledge enclosed within this book.

Work Your Quirks has it all, written in a witty and conversational style and packed full of practical tips that you can put into action immediately, it's a book that I will refer to all Happenistas, women who want to make things happen in their unique way!"

Jenny Garrett, Award Winning Coach, Author and Speaker

"Work your Quirks is and should be the upwardly mobile lady's handbook for 2017 and beyond. If you didn't know and were curious about the meaning of personal branding then "Voila!" there it is.

The writing is eloquent yet understandable, with quirky funny bits which women from all walks of life will identify with.

The businesswoman's companion for a sparkling personal brand is exactly what it says it is."

Candy Kisseih
International Journalist & Host of The Kiki Chat Show

"Work Your Quirks is a book that's very easy to read without any jargon or unrealistic targets. It's straight forward and very engaging. Every woman needs this on their bedside table to refer to every day and use as their go-to book of sparkling gems!"

Caroline Morgan
Founder of Caroline Rosanna Life Coaching

MAIN CONTRIBUTORS

FOREWORD
Penny Power OBE

ILLUSTRATIONS
Amanda Quartey (Wardrobe – Chapter 7)

STAGE 1: RESEARCH
Helen Walbey (Potential of Women Entrepreneurs)

STAGE 2: REVIEW
Mavis Amankwah (Press Relations)

STAGE 3: REVEAL
Stella Fehmi (Successful Networking)

STAGE 4: REFINE
Rachel McGuinness (Health & Wellness)

PUBLISHING CONSULTANT
Sarah Houldcroft (Goldcrest Books)

CONTENTS

FOREWORD

It is an era of self-discovery, self-employment and unselfishness! Never before have we been in a time of such transparency and the desire for trust. *Work your Quirks* is a timely and highly relevant book for anyone that wants to be known, liked and trusted.

Your brand has to ooze trust. Trust is an asset we can all build. Building genuine trust that is not purely managed within a marketing and branding office is the tough part, it cannot be designed, delegated or manufactured.

Every one of us must build trust, and as Lily says, this comes from a deep process of knowing yourself and having the integrity and genuine passion about what you, your company and your brand oozes and provides. Brand-YOU.

The need to learn how to build a brand is not a luxury, being part of the new connected world and using your heart as much as your head is a skill and must become part of who you are. Your brand is who you are as much as what you do.

Work your Quirks takes you on a journey of discovering what makes you sparkle, and how to enable others to feel that and consume it. What a great plan to go through, a set of skills that will become part of you for the rest of your life. It will absorb your stress, keep you fired up and help you to get out of bed even when you felt battered and bruised from your day when you got into bed.

I wish everyone great success in this wonderful, connected, transparent world, where the good rise and the bad get no attention at all.

Penny Power OBE

Founder and CEO of The Business Cafe

INTRODUCTION

If I had been given a book like this at the beginning of my entrepreneurial journey a decade ago, my business would have moved along so much more quickly in terms of the things I wanted to achieve. I know you are very busy with clients and customers demanding your attention, not to mention marketing, admin, staff, contractors, and the like, so I thought a concise and straight to the point book you can carry in your Louis Vuitton, might be just the ticket.

This book is for those who want to start their businesses, or those who are already in business and want to know how the heck to build a personal brand. The good news is that you already have one—we all do. So stop fretting about it, OK? The trick is whether we recognise its enormous power by working with the best elements to get us what we want for ourselves and our businesses. As businesswomen, we are firing on all cylinders and the weird and wonderful thing called social media has made it all the more complex. 10 years ago if anyone had said to me that surfing the net and checking my Instagram account would have been stressful, I would have said 'Shut the front door!'

Today, it's the reality we all face and we can liken it to the days of yore when one didn't have the right mix-tape! But not to worry, I'm all about positivity and I shy away from the fearmongers who tell you if you don't do this, you won't get that. I'm a firm believer that this process is serious fun – in that we must take it seriously but have fun whilst doing it. In a nutshell, I believe you can have a sparkling personal brand that will be worthy of note! We will walk through what I call Working your QUIRKs – an acronym that I've developed over my years as a brand specialist for some famous and some infamous brands to decipher the abstract concept we refer to as a personal brand. Quirky, for me means Quality, Unique, Integrity, Realistic and Kind to Yourself. This book will give you ideas to get your best mix-tape to rival your friends and neighbours and you get to play it out loud and boogie to it too. And as if that wasn't enough, we are going to work with some serious blingy diamonds a lot in this book.

We will follow a similar process to manufacturing and selling of diamonds from mine to shop-floor and beyond. Like diamonds, our personal brands already exist, often hidden under tons of dirt per carat of diamond found – quality is few and far between. Did you know that only one in a million diamonds are quality one-carat stones, and only one in five million are two-carat?[1] Imagine your brand as a diamond in the special one or two carat category. That is what we'd like to achieve when we speak about a personal brand that sparkles. Given the choice, I'd want to be in the rare more valuable range, so that I could command the very best price – wouldn't you?

With the explosion of the internet, our brands are now competing with over 3 billion people on the internet[2] not to mention our offline activities which cannot be ignored.

Come, let's have fun whilst we get to grips with our personal brands that only we have the copyright to. My hope is that as you read *Work your Quirks*, you make notes as appropriate and jump back in every now and then just to pick up bits and pieces because a great personal brand is not built in a day. It requires a series of daily tweaks to stay fresh, relevant and compelling. This is where being quirky really improves your brand promise.

Oh and one last thing; if you see ( ) in the text, like the ones on the previous page, then you will find all the info you need in the References and Resources section on page 158.

CHAPTER 1

Work your Q.U.I.R.Ks – Preamble to a Sparkling Brand

Q = Quality

U = Unique

I = Integrity

R = Realistic

K = Kind to Yourself

Some have asked how you start with your personal brand and others have said, "I'm so confused about this. Does it have anything to do with my business, too?" The straight answer is yes. Your private, personal, professional and public images are all about you first, before your business, so it makes sense to think of them as the same. They are not mutually exclusive. I should know, because to me the notion of personal branding can appear lofty at first. After over 10 years in the game, I am still learning new tips and tricks.

I've employed the acronym QUIRKs as illustrated above with a notion that we all have some quirks that will make us stand out. I believe that those quirks are what will lead us to the holy grail of the ever-elusive strong personal brand. Not everyone will like those quirks, but I guess we are not here to serve and please all, are we? A handful is plenty as long as we serve them to the very best of our ability and do it with aplomb! Let's explore each one a bit further.

Quality – If we think of ourselves as brands, then we must ask ourselves whether we want our product to be a questionable imitation of the real thing, with a generic label, gathering dust on the clearance rack at the discount store... or do we want our product to be the gold standard, featured in the window of the finest store in town? Obviously we'd all prefer to be the latter, but what I know for sure, is that how quality is defined, is not always up to us alone. We must consider the perceptions of those we want to influence, because ultimately our brands are held in their hearts and minds too.

Unique – Only you can do "you" flawlessly; that's my mantra. If we were all the same, life would be boring. So think of the one thing (talent, skill, ability, or connection) that you possess, unique to you, that no one else in your circle, network, or profession can lay claim to. That's your quirk, so work it like Julia Roberts on Rodeo Drive in *Pretty Woman*... OK, I've seen that movie one too many times.

Integrity – Unless we have armies of PR gurus readily available to wipe away any smudge that threatens to tarnish our professional images, we need to carefully guard our brands with integrity. Being trustworthy, being transparent, and delivering what we promise means our brands will be perceived as a top-notch products worthy of note. We must also remember as well that the other brands we associate with will rub off on our own, so it may be worthwhile to do an annual review of our immediate network, to see which brands are working in sync with ours.

Realistic – The constant pursuit of perfection can stifle creativity. Given that times and trends are moving so quickly, we can no longer afford to over-analyse and tinker with great ideas, as we look for the perfect opportunity before we present them. We have to be realistic with the time and resources that we have. If we can face ourselves in the mirror knowing we've done our absolute best with what we had available, that's good enough. Let's just step out.

Kind-to-Yourself – My favourite one. Today we are pulled in so many directions that we tend to forget we are only human, and occasionally must gear down in order to rev back up. We are often our own worst critics. Being kind to others can be easy, but giving ourselves a break is easier said than done. This notion, to me, is one of the lesser-known personal branding tricks because if we are chilled, relaxed, and refreshed -- our brands are more likely to sparkle.

THE 4 STAGES OF BRANDING

Now, let's look at you, through the 4 stages of branding with diamonds as a theme. Since these precious stones are a girl's best friend, we will be using the process of mining to depict the development of your personal brand. I love diamonds myself, but had never really known how they were made until last year when I was asked to speak at an International Women's Conference in Spain. Topics were personal branding and LinkedIn. The idea was to marry the two. Of course, I thought, marriage – ring and compatibility. Diamonds naturally started to develop in my mind. That meant me having to really do my research to see how these wonderful gems are unearthed, made, sold and so on. I found it quite fascinating as a businesswoman mainly because of the processes followed in the mining world. You see, for me, if I have a process I'm less likely to go off-piste and mess things up. This also meant I could easily have something that I could refer to that resonated with my audience. These stages of personal branding with diamonds are presented here in 4 sections:

◊ **Research** – where we dig deep to unearth the diamond;

◊ **Review** – where we go through what we've found and how we manage it;

◊ **Reveal** – is about the manufacturing and creation of the new gem and finally;

◊ **Refine** – where we take our fabulous selves to the finest shop in town, sell our brand story and maintain its sparkle and glitter long after the sale is done.

In the end the perfect diamond shouldn't be kept hidden because we have to ask ourselves, why then have we bothered to create it in the first place? Every gem, within a perfect setting, must be displayed well and be shown to the world. Brand-YOU is no different.

Talking about processes, opposite is a snapshot of the personal branding stages I've developed to get that personal brand sparkling continually.

STAGE 1: RESEARCH

Preparing to mine your brand promise

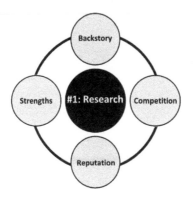

Diamonds are one of the oldest items you will ever own because they have been under the ground for centuries. In fact, they are part of nature, but unless we dig and mine for them, we will never discover them and hold them in our hands. It takes time and effort to turn them into the beautiful stones that we all know and love. We are also in a sense the oldest version of ourselves that we know. For instance, if you are 40 years old, you will only know yourself for 40 years – not 41 and not 39 so you and no one else will know you better than you do.

Of course only you have your own brand story that only you can tell authentically. It's your narrative which you can play and write any way you want. In unearthing the diamond, though, we have to prepare, set the scene, and have a plan and direction as to how the unearthing process will be. Some might say, "Why don't you just get yourself some new suits and business cards?" Those tactics will work for a while, sure, but without a much deeper excavation, the rebranding process will be shallow and might produce only lacklustre results, rendering the process worthless at best and counter-productive at worst. But we are not doing scare mongering here – we are going to look at how best to get the brand on track and in the right light in order to sparkle.

CHAPTER 2

Your brand promise

> *Preparation, I have often said, is rightly two-thirds of any venture.*
> **Amelia Earhart**

YOUR BACK STORY

Did you know that to produce a one-carat diamond, miners must use pipes of about 3500 feet deep and roughly 200 tonnes of sand, and other minerals will have to be unearthed? Only 20% will be suitable to be polished and the rest will be used for industrial purposes. As much as we are not doing deep mine excavation, mining our brand promise is not dissimilar. To decide where we want to go, we have to dig really deep.

Just as mining companies don't get up suddenly to rush down the mine-shaft, neither should we begin our process without doing a bit of research to see where we are. In the early part of the process which is pretty much research driven, many often think that this step is unnecessary because we might believe that we already know what our brands represent. Try to take a step back to review your brand as it stands today. This can be via various methods. I do this every 18 months or so. This is one of the most fundamental steps in the process and as famous pilot Amelia Earhart stated, *"Preparation, I have often said, is rightly two-thirds of any venture."* Try to find out what people think about you when you are not around. As basic as it appears, that's it. What are you giving off and how are people receiving it? If you were to ask your friends, family, clients and associates what three words describe you, would they all use the same words? A wide variety of responses might suggest that there is some inconsistency and one of the biggest Cs in branding is Consistency. That, my friend, is what we are after. Managing your brand allows you to lead the conversation about you. Whether we like it or not, people will talk. So why don't we give them the right things to talk about? You are then leading your brand campaign.

There are various tools to use to start the conversation about where your brand is now, right now. One thing I would strongly recommend is to only solicit responses from those who know you well, wish you well and will be objective and not use this as a tool to beat you up. A gut feel will point you in the direction of who the right people are. Not just the sycophants either – choose straight-talking people who have something of value to add to your message. Below are a handful of options to consider for researching the brand called YOU:

360Reach Personal Branding Survey
www.reachcc.com/360v5register

One of my favourite and trusted surveys is the 360Reach. The first and leading personal branding survey. It enables you to understand how you are perceived by those around you. It has been used by nearly a million career-minded professionals and entrepreneurs and has been incorporated into talent development programs in 20% of Fortune 100 companies.

You can send to pretty much anyone, family, friends, boss, client, associate, you name it and you can analyse it. I certainly use it myself and also for my clients. It goes far beyond the basic client/boss questionnaire and even to fun questions like if you were a car what would you be and why? If you fancy something different then why not? Add your own spin to it in order to differentiate yourself. I absolutely love the tool, have used it for over 10 years and would highly recommend it.

SurveyMonkey: www.surveymonkey.com/

Create a free account with 10 questions. Whatever you do, make the survey anonymous as most people will be more honest if they feel it won't be held against them. I have included a few of my own suggestions to get you started in the table over the page. They are not exhaustive – add your own questions, by all means, and why not have a go at answering them yourself first.

Telephone and/or face to face feedback

This will be a perfect opportunity to meet those you haven't spoken to properly in a while. Ask them out for coffee or teleconference, using the various media available – easier if video is involved if it's a remote affair and you get to have eye contact. Skype and Zoom come to mind. Let them know you are conducting a survey for your personal and business development and you would love their input because their opinion means a lot to you. Meet with a group of no more than five people at a time. Too many will be hard to manage unless you have a team with you. You can see it as an online brand party and could also be a networking opportunity for others.

Survey Questions Example

Use these questions and/or create your own

	Question	Answer
1	4 Adjectives that describe me	
2	My top 4 strengths	
3	Top 4 skills	
4	4 words would describe what's special about me	
5	If I had an ideal career what would it be?	
6	My 4 business brand attributes: e.g. Name - catchy or bland, Logo - bold, Personality - warm, Pricing - exclusive	
7	What are my potential growth areas? (maximum of 4)	
8		
9		
10		

You offline

Our reputation is who we are, really. This should not be our carefully choreographed online personas, cropped and photoshopped within an inch of our lives. No, this is us in the mirror – no filter. Us, in the mirror looking dead straight and saying who are we and what do we want to achieve? We could call this the strategy development session with key elements such as:

◊ Where we are

◊ Where we are going

◊ Who we need

◊ How we will get there

◊ **What we will do when we get there**

Let's remember that only a tiny percentage of business revenue comes from online activity. Experts say 5% or less, so for now we will leave that bit out completely. In my view, the online world provides a false sense of security and purpose because it's new and changes pretty much by the hour. Let's focus on the bricks and mortar part of your brand, meaning you in the flesh and your business offline. What are your current offerings?

◊ What are your potential areas of growth as an individual and as a business leader? Your brand strategy should have an aspirational approach – which you can liken to the adage of dressing for the job you want, not the job you have.

◊ What scares you but will make you a leader in your field? Could it be writing your own book, perhaps? (Or at least an e-book.) Or how about public speaking? I know it's one of the greatest fears of many people, especially women, since we are judged on so many different fronts from our expertise, our clothes to even our jewellery. It makes perfect sense that some of us would rather have a root canal done than speak in front of a crowd. Fear not! The more you do it, the more confident you become. Or you could get yourself a coach. I used webinars to cut my teeth into the speaking game, and there's no reason why you too cannot use something that is small in scale and build up gradually. With webinars, you can hide behind a screen too until you get more confident.

◊ A wardrobe update might also be in the cards because if, like me, your weight fluctuates up and down 10 pounds or so, your wardrobe may be heaving with clothes for different seasons and different sizes. We will cover this extensively in section 3. You cannot rebrand without covering this bit and it's particularly important because as women we have a double whammy; judging one another and having others judge us. We must learn to be more forgiving of ourselves. As warm and fuzzy as that might feel, this is in fact essential to a brand that will sparkle when confidence is second nature.

CHAPTER 3

Preparing to discover your sparkle
What makes you stand out?

In this chapter we are going to explore what you can do to help you stand out from others around you. What are your core assets? We will look at the reputation and strengths of Brand-YOU. Going into this detail now will help form the foundation of your sparkle as we dig deep and extract some real gems. If you are going to stand out you need to know from who and what so we will also be looking at your competition. Who are they, what do they do? For even more help later on in the chapter, I will be calling on female entrepreneur extraordinaire, Helen Walbey, to share her views on being an entrepreneur in a man's world.

Reputation: What do people say about you when you are not around?

The Internet has brought about a truckload of experts, I must say. Do you feel deluged by it all? I do, but I have learned to keep the overnight stars as learning objects rather than objects of desire. Everyone's journey is different and as my friend recently told me, we are all writing different exam papers in our personal and professional lives, so looking over my shoulder to get your answers may not give you the grade you want. This was real food for thought. Studying for your own exam then means having a clear idea of what your potential questions in the exam will be and if you are writing a chemistry paper then you should be reading the chemistry book, not looking over the algebra questions for inspiration. Makes sense, doesn't it?

So here we are, almost at the mineshaft of our brand promise, with the lights on and the diamond ore about to be unearthed. What we find may be full of unnecessary things that we do not have the time nor the expertise to deal with straight away. If time is of the essence, accentuate the positives, I say. Other stones might also be in the fray. Let's not throw them all away, as they might be essential to the development process. These will position us as separate from other brands. It will be part of our arsenal of tools that we could work with in the future in our brand make-over bag.

In the prep stage we will now begin to define what we have found in the mine and start to separate the important bits, at a very high level and here are ideas to get us started:

1. Top strengths – those that you can wake up on a Saturday morning and do without thinking about whether you will be paid for or not. That's the motivational skill we want. You might be the best baker but online investment is what you're really passionate about and in this example online investment will be your motivational skill. That's what will make your pupils dilate just thinking about doing it.

2. Top areas that you want to stop doing – burn-out skills such as the baker above; These are things you are good at but don't enjoy doing very much yet they may pay the bills. Finding a way to off-load these

can make a huge difference to you and your brand. That said, if they pay the bills, I'd go very slowly. I don't want you to go bankrupt in pursuit of your motivational skills. It has to be measured against your financial and career reality.

3. People you can call upon to support you – behind every successful woman is a bevy of sheroes holding her up. Find your sheroes – engage with them. Some will be at your beck and call and others you might have to find as you continue with your rebranding exercise.

4. Culling – this is the opportunity to really take stock of the things that enhance your growth and those that deplete it. It has to be a very honest time with yourself or a coach if you have one. Get one anyway; it's the best accessory you could ever purchase for your brand. Now, I must warn you that the culling process is not done overnight but it is planned and on paper – who and what will you cull for the next stage of your brand development? You can't take everything with you if you are going to create new and exciting things, can you? Agile, svelte and portable is going to be our new message. Adaptable even, though before we can do that there's the rather interesting thing called competition. Some think of it as an ugly word but to me that's good.

Healthy competition, that is because you are not going to be competing on the negative – it's positive all the way. Selling on people's fears is short-lived. You want to be seen to be the one that people want to buy from because they believe you have something special that will improve the things they already have. They want greater things for themselves, not from lack but from a place of abundance. Let's therefore look at the healthy completion and how we go about deciding which and what we should look out for in the competition.

Profiling the competition:

As strange as this might sound, it is vital to know who your competition is; otherwise you will be woman-marking every person who so much as whispers that they do what you do. Just because they say so or they have been mentioned in one press or another that they are the go-to person in say business architecture or life coaching. No – let's break it down a little bit because your competition starts first with you. Who you are, what you are good at and everything we've said earlier. So for instance let's look at the life coaches out there – and I will use LinkedIn as my yardstick as many professionals are reportedly hanging out there, though later on I'll introduce you to some other professional networks that might work for you. As we have several life coaches out there – 70,000 on LinkedIn alone, it's virtually impossible to see all of them as competition, you will surely feel overwhelmed. Did I say personal branding gives you wings in that it brings you confidence to take on more challenges? OK, back to this book. You get to map out who the competition is against our own strengths. Let's have a little exercise about getting clarity on your competition. First of all, as crazy as it sounds, give them a name – not a name that you know but an abstract name – let's say her name is Venus and this is what she might say about herself and her business:

"I'm a coach, I'm a mind-set coach, I work with young adults, I work with young adults who are women in care, I work with young adult women from bereaved homes who are now in care to help them through the bereavement process and rebuild their lives for what will no doubt be a tough future ahead." If you are one who works with women in high flying jobs you will be looking at the wrong competition. In essence our competition should mirror what we do or at the very least have an arsenal of bravado that when we stand toe to toe with, there is something to compare rather those who may be lesser than we are or have nothing in common with where we are heading, and we either want to beat them in a friendly sparring way or whose shoulders we want to stand on. Let's look at those sort of areas we want to look at in determining our, realistic competition.

This example comes from my early days as a fresh marketing and branding virgin at Arthur Andersen – we felt that none of the other top firms could hold a candle to us. We were mavericks, even our literature was risqué and I remember clearly when we did a fabulous campaign with 'crystal balls', how the eyebrows went up in accounting and consulting circles. How can accountants start talking about balls – they would ask, but you know what, it got us to be seen as separate from number-crunching nerdy brands with no real differentiation. Blue, white and black colours were the norm. We weighed in with orange together with other bold colours. We had an edge to us that those clients who were looking for something else wanted. Of course, there have been some mergers, acquisitions and downright scandals that have made the top four. We were part of the big five and would only compete with the big five – and that was very much about staying in our lane. There were projects that we couldn't be seen to be taking on and just couldn't because the client didn't have the resources to work with us or we didn't have all the know how to work with the client. We outsourced or said no. As much as things are changing, the old-school rules still apply. I know today, big firms have to compete with smaller firms in order to be seen to be agile and scalable but don't let that fool you. The small firms do not have the big bank of cash that big firms can throw at problems and challenges. They do so with big bucks and will not lose out too quickly, therefore it makes sense to weigh up the competition carefully before you start targeting their audience in order to make a quick buck. Let's now look at key areas of competition profiling.

The key areas of competition profiling

The table opposite represents the key questions to ask yourself when you are thinking about your competitors. Take a look at them and write your answers in the space provided. This will help you build up a profile of your competitors.

Now that we know who Ms Competition is, she is the one we need to watch as we grow. I have seen many who have said they are this and that and it may not necessarily be true. The message for you is to be present and focused on building your personal brand where you can be seen as the specialist in a particular area. Having an area of expertise and being seen to be *the go-to-person* is one of the most important things you can own, apart from education, of course. Being the go-to will take you so far, but you also want to deliver exceptionally well so when the next opportunity comes, you will be on top of their minds. You will be their BAE – Before Anyone Else. They will refer, and showcase what you can do without you paying a penny in marketing effort. The brand that works for you when you are asleep is the best kind. Perhaps you can begin to see your brand as part of your sales force – selling on cue and in your sleep.

We love competition because they give us something that we may not have but aspire to and also know what they represent. If it's similar, that's good but as much as none of our fingers are similar, there is likely to be something that they do not provide nor have expertise in that we can capitalise

Think about your competitors

In which industry and sector are they most prevalent?	
Do they inspire you? What is the point – personal branding is about aspirational goals so if people do not inspire you, why chase after them or even compare yourself to them? Not everyone who makes a lot of noise out there will inspire you	
What are they doing similar to you? Coaching, event planning, speakers etc	
What is the competition doing differently?	
Could you do some of their different things better?	
Will they be happy to collaborate? As women, we are more open to collaboration if we speak the same language of win/win	
What are their weaknesses? They may not be confident as a speaker or be social media savvy	
Can you fill in on their weaknesses? Speak, if that's the last thing to do	
Are they seen as an expert for what you do? Experts are two a penny in my book. Specialists are more rounded	

on. It's definitely a process worth going through to see what opportunities present themselves to you.

My differentiator is that as much as I can craft a Branded LinkedIn Makeover and consult on website and logo development to give the brand direction, I'm also really passionate about having the wardrobe tied to my offering and I believe that in itself is a unique combination that few of my competitors have. Looking and sounding the part means we are 50% there.

What is so special about you? Your key strengths

Use the VIA institute (www.viacharacter.org/www/Character-Strengths-Survey) to test out your character strengths and plot your highlights below. Again, I'd recommend using your top 5 strengths and use those to direct your brand qualities. If you are a social animal and are asked to do something in a straight-jacket way, then you are not showcasing your strengths enough. Use the table below to write down your character strengths.

Top 5 strengths

What are your strengths?	How and where will you use them?

CHAPTER 3

During the writing process, I caught up with another shero of mine, Helen Walbey, MD of Recycle Scooters and National Policy Chair for Health and Diversity at the Federation of Small Businesses to shine some light on her views about the female entrepreneur especially as one in a male dominated industry. This was done in an interview style, similar to my *Tea with Lily* radio interviews and these are the highlights:

Lily talking to Helen Walbey - Female Entrepreneurs

Lily: Based on the research you have done with the FSB and the report *'Women in Enterprise: The Untapped Potential'*, what would be your advice to help women, particularly entrepreneurs in moving forward with their personal brands?

Helen: When starting my business in a mature market I needed to find a place where I could stand out and ensure my voice was heard. Motorcycle salvage is a male dominated sector and I knew this could be a real disadvantage for me with regard to business credibility and exploring new opportunities so I had to find a way to use these disadvantages to my advantage. The way I found to do this was to emphasise my difference, not hide it. I developed my personal brand around the fact I was a woman in a male industry so I was going to stand out. I just made sure I *really* stood out.

Today only one in five UK businesses are majority women owned, so I know I could become a trailblazer and help support other women. Women led businesses contribute over £75 billion to the UK economy but if we set up businesses at the same rate as men we could add another £10 billion. That is a lot of untapped potential.

I am confident and I used that to carve out a voice in my industry even when people assumed I was the receptionist or tea maker. They quickly understood that, in fact, I led the business and was the main decision maker and strategist. This was not easy at the start and I had to keep banging on doors for some time before I got them all open.

Lily: Where can we tap into the support out there?

Helen: 40% of women business owners still do not get support from external sources and there are a variety of reasons for this. Part of it can be down to confidence, part of it can be down to actually knowing what support is available in your area and part of it can then be accessing that support, particularly in rural areas where there is poor or no broadband signal. This can risk under-capitalising your business when you start up. This can impact not just at the start up stage but right through the life cycle of the business and can restrict your ability to grow your business. Women on average start their businesses with a third less capital than their male counterparts and tend to start businesses in sectors where there are already many other businesses and less opportunity to make significant profits.

However there is good news too. When you account for sector and age, women led businesses out-perform male led ones so we are able to succeed in business and we are able to grow, we just need to be able to do it in a more diverse range of industries.

Lily: What are your top tips for personal branding success?

Helen: Find your Q.U.I.R.K. when you know what makes you tick, what your core values are and what you are actually in business for, you can find the point of what you do. When you know your Q.U.I.R.K.s then you can find ways to exploit them, turn weaknesses into strengths and threats into opportunities to find new ways of doing business or new markets to do your business in.

Find a compatible and effective mentor and identify who your role models are; they do not have to be in business but those people who inspire you to keep going. They might be your mum or the leader of a nation, but they can help drive you forward into the opportunities that are awaiting you.

Lily: What can the government etc. do for us women in business?

Helen: There are rafts of measures that the Federation of Small Businesses identified in its report 'Women in Enterprise – The Untapped Potential'. These include:

- Improving women's knowledge of the full range of finance options available to them. This is particularly relevant with regard to alternative forms of finance like angel investment and venture capital.

- There is an opportunity to highlight the full range of support that is currently available on the 'Business is Great' website. It has a page dedicated to women in business yet knowledge of this site is low amongst women.

- There is also a real opportunity when it comes to procurement and supply chains. Larger tier one suppliers could be contracted to have diversity written into their supply chains, as they do in America. This would begin to level the playing field for women-led businesses and open up opportunities for accelerated growth.

- More visible and diverse role models can also help inspire other women into a career in business and enterprise, as you can't be what you can't see. Wales already has a successful programme with 350 role models that has been running in schools, colleges and universities for the last ten years. This helps inspire younger people to broaden their horizons and open up enterprise to them.

- Lastly, equalising maternity pay for the self-employed will make a difference to women who will not have to return to work so quickly after having children.

- I know when I started in business it was difficult to see women working in atypical sectors and the industry was portrayed in a very macho way. This is changing and the world of enterprise is opening up but it has not been easy and there is a very long way still to go. The work of organisations like the Federation of Small Businesses and Facebook with their global #SheMeansBusiness campaign all help as do all the women out there who are already in business who stand up and help bring about the change they want to see.

I am lucky I have sought out and found some excellent mentors who have helped guide me to achieve what I have in business and I look for inspiration in all the amazing women I meet but I never go it alone and that collaboration and companionship has helped me get through the rough patches and become successful in my field.

STAGE 2: REVIEW

Your brand promise in review; Prepping and primping

Once the diamond has been unearthed, it needs to be equally prepped and sorted. That is so that the metaphorical wheat is separated from the chaff where the real gems are presented to the diamond market. Whereupon the not so special ones are sold on for industrial purposes. I bet like me you'd like your brand to be among those that will be picked and sent off to the markets. And why not? Did you know diamonds have around 5,000 different categories and prices and these are sorted with 10 sites held each year?

This is no different from brands – different brands can sell the same products but its quality, how it is prepared, marketed and presented, that will make a difference. Imagine that as one of the 5,000, you will want to make the final cut amongst that top group. That's where your personal brand should be aiming for. Better still where there are 10 sites each year lasting a week, where private buyers are invited to private auctions, we want to be one of those diamonds for sure where people are bidding for our products and services and we can really name our price or decide perhaps not. Great, don't you think? In this section, I will talk about brand direction and look at what angle to start making waves in your industry or sector as a brand that stands out for all the right reasons.

CHAPTER 4

Perhaps when we find ourselves wanting everything,
it is because we are dangerously close to
wanting nothing.
Sylvia Plath

There are those who might be very happy to go along with the next big thing and there are those who say, OK, it's the next big thing but is it right for me, right now? That's what I'd like to think most people fall into and if you are one of the latter, then great. If you are still trying to decide which way you are swaying then let's look at the very first signpost that will decide your brand direction – Setting goals for Brand -YOU because it's something you can refer to at the end of the year or the timeline you've set for yourself.

As a serious business woman you would have set some goals of some description, whether written on a Post-it or in a carefully colour-coded notebook or simply filed in your head under the must-do compartment of goals. It doesn't matter, not all are born to be organised from day one. Some of us follow our noses first and then look at the map later while others will plan everything. Whichever one you are, it's all good – we do not beat ourselves up in Personal Branding, ever!

In building your brand there are many areas that might concern you. For instance, am I building for my personal image or am I building for my business? The answer should always be for both simultaneously. We are our own best billboards that don't need to be commissioned to be aired only during primetime TV. It's a daily invitation for you to stand out from the crowd so here are some pointers on how to get the GPS set up for your brand.

Your GPS: Guiding principles, passions and strategy

To give your brand direction though, you will have to turn on your built-in GPS to put you in the best position to compete effectively. The notion of the GPS here, relates to (a) *Guiding principles* that keep you sane on a crazy day, (b) *Passions* that make you tick, and (c) a *Strategy* to improve your chances of brand success. Let's take each in turn.

Guiding principles: These are often set in stone which, together, form the beacon for your brand. These could include attention to detail, respect for others, community engagement, entrepreneurship, even innovation. They become the indelible ink that runs through everything you do ensuring that your professional, private, personal qualities are always interlinked and therefore never mutually exclusive.

Passions: What floats your boat and what gets your goat? Both questions will point you in one direction only. For example, if lack of diversity awareness gets your goat then you are likely to be passionate about promoting diversity within the business environment. When your guiding principles and passions meet, greater opportunities are no longer accidental but on purpose.

Strategy: Are you a fun-loving person who loves to be surrounded by people? Why not ask to join your business or community group's social committee? A bean counter by trade? Then supporting or being a treasurer at a charity of your choice could be as easy as 1, 2, 3. What about the fashion forward individual? Dazzling those around you by donating your time and offering wardrobe advice to other business women could be just the ticket. What you stand for and how you translate these into everyday activities will play a major role in managing your brand. One does, however, need tenacity and a great support network.

Navigate and highlight what's important to get your best self out there. Would it be for instance where you present yourself to the world and how you do so? I'd choose a maximum of 10 areas of focus over a 3-year period. Once upon a time, goals were set for the longer term but at the rate at which things are moving anything longer than 3 years may well be obsolete anyway so why waste time over complicating what you might not be able to control by planning around it? Let's be more realistic and look at the short term - 6 months, medium term - 18 months and 3 years will be the long term.

The key to great goal-setting is dumping all your thoughts into one long list. These might include the following:

Review logo: Is your brand identity hanging on the right signpost?

Redesign business cards: Any vital changes should be reviewed.

Review your online activities: where are your potential clients hanging out? Go there.

Rebranding: Let your contacts know that you are rebranding.

Wardrobe review & update: Purposeful choices for business.

Headshots: Is your look current? If older than 3 years, we need to get you an update.

Speaking: Helps to increased visibility and ultimately, profit.

Writing: Be seen as a specialist in your field of expertise.

Review competitive landscape: What's coming up and prepare for friendly combat.

Repackage offering: What can you add or take out to repackage for clients?

Signature products: Craft your own signature line of products.

Charitable giving: Wear your heart on your sleeve with time, cash or both.

Personal brand statement: Punchy and simple with a strapline.

So you have the GPS at the ready, you have mapped out your route to a glittering business success, bravo. Now we have to look at what makes us so special among other people and whom we want to attract to the brand fest.

CHAPTER 5

Finding the ideal target

Some of the things we have to do in determining brand direction can be downright boring, to say the least, and targeting for me is one of them. It is worth it in the end, so let's just roll with it, shall we?

I want to work with people who get me. Don't you? I know when you are starting it's not so easy, and you may be tempted to take all and sundry who throw their hard-earned cash at you, but between you and me, targeting is one of the less used secrets of branding. It's the holy grail of client yumminess. Don't you want those buyers to say, "I love to buy from Minerva because…. [Fill in the blanks]"

And they may well fill the profile of Ms Competition whom we call Venus, but may want more which she may not be able to provide. Just because they are a client/customer, doesn't mean that they do not have aspirations like you. The trick is putting yourself in their shoes. Ask yourself if they would fit. If not, they may not be the right fit for your business either. My naughty older brother once said to me, if it fits like a glove, it must be love, and I believe he had a point. Of course he was talking about something else but it's really the same principle.

So whose metaphorical glove do you think you might fit into?

Age – It could be the young and trendy millennials or the experienced and wealthy baby boomers. The needs of both groups will differ tremendously. There will be a slew of offerings for each target audience but the trick is to speak to each group alone and not be too much of a generalist. Niching is an ideal way to do this, which we will explore further later on in this chapter.

Profession or business – what do they do for a living? First though, you may find those who are working for someone else may not want to change their profession and that's fine. Even in the current economic climate where they work and who they work for represents their career. Can you work with those in a particular industry? For instance, if you are a financial advisor who specialises in helping doctors, places where they congregate in huge numbers must be one of your playgrounds too. You have to find a reason to be in their midst and understand their language. You go where your clients hang out. Doctors are now seen as strategy developers especially if they are GPs running a practice. You may wish to differentiate further between the GP and the consultant paediatrician, for example.

What do they do for fun? – So much is under-estimated about the things that we do for fun and we tend to look at the things that are money generating. Basically what do you think makes your yummy target client feel happy when there's no money to be earned? Me, I'm still looking for a golf partner – my family cannot stand it, and I love it and would welcome someone trying to pair me up with a newish golf enthusiast with nothing but a good swing. That's me. Would I be your ideal client if you were into golf yourself? It's also the lifestyle things that we forget about when we look at what others are doing outside of work. This may include their disposable income, and what they choose to do with it might give us a clue about the things that make them smile.

Relevance – Where will you most likely sell your brand and to whom? How relevant is what you are offering to those customers who might be willing to buy from you? Just because you are promoting your business doesn't mean that you will get customers straight away. They go through several stages before they get to part with their hard earned cash.

The customer buying cycle in marketing terms is replicated on page 52 to allow you to see how you might position your brand. The AIDA model, developed by Kotler, a marketing guru in academia, shows how we go through a series of emotions before we take actions.

Customer Satisfaction – If customer is happy, they come back for more or tell others. If they are not happy, they tell others and never come back. We therefore must follow up and ensure that the post purchase experience is a positive one.

If a purchase decision is made, we may have one more step or a series of steps to follow through and that's where customer satisfaction chimes in. This is by far one of the greatest ways to get repeat custom. Aftercare is as important as the sale itself. Recommendations then follow on from there if you have done your follow up and follow through very well.

We as business owners must also be aware of this and not feel that each touch point with the customer/client will result immediately in a sale. No, it's a long process. You might even find that if you get the sale too quickly, there might be some attachment to it, such as the client not knowing what they have bought. Expectations might be different, but if they go through all the stages before they buy, they would have done

The AIDA model

Awareness

To raise awareness of the brand to our target audience who at this stage will come from a large pool of potential buyers

Interest

This is our opportunity to educate and inform our target of the benefits of doing business with us and of course our raison d'etre, the reason for our brand's existence

Desire

This is when our promotional prowess and tactics will then engage further with a by then smaller pool of potential buyers

Action

A decision made and carried through by taking action to either buy or walk away but an action is made one way or another their own analysis of what they expect and they are more likely to be satisfied with the purchase decision.

In the end, your brand will always remain in the hearts and minds of the target audience and the emotional connection that they attach to it. The AIDA model is used extensively in marketing and promotional strategies and I believe branding is no different.

Competitive edge with a PR Plan

Having a personal PR plan means that you are immediately predisposed to propel yourself into the press at any given time. One of my Sheroes, Mavis Amankwah, speaks eloquently on the subject and her book, *44 Ways to Grow Your Business or Brand* gives a step-by-step guide to increase profits. She says and I quote:

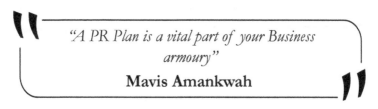

"A PR Plan is a vital part of your Business armoury"
Mavis Amankwah

On the following pages, Mavis shares her nuggets of wisdom on the power of PR and how to make it work for you.

Mavis Amankwah - The Power of PR

"What is PR?" you ask. The Chartered Institute of Public Relations says: *"Public Relations is about reputation - the result of what you do, what you say and what others say about you."*

Planning is key so that you know what you are supposed to do, what it will cost in time and money, what the results are likely to be, how you implement and how you are going to measure the results. Evaluating can be a challenge when your tactics are multi-dimensional and that's why you need to keep the goals SMART and make sure there are lots of BHAGs – Big Huge Audacious Goals!

BHAGs include your targeting efforts and it's not just about which clients but also which media and which industry so you can craft your message accordingly. I look at vertical media, which is media from the same sector or lifestyle where you can use current studies, yours included, to build a campaign to raise your profile.

When you decide on PR, it should not just be about quick wins – it should be with the long game in mind for developing your business. It is a marketing tool and not an alternative to advertising. The two go hand in hand and neither is a one-off activity and in simple terms it's a media game.

Right angles for the press: To get into the press you need the right angles with a media plan which can be done on a spreadsheet – doesn't have to be fancy, as long as you and those you work with understand the content. Make a list of titles you'd like to see your stories in, their contact details and deadlines which you can get from the media titles directly.

Below are some angles you could use:

- A milestone in business
- Winning an award
- Tips and advice
- Publicity stunts
- Celebrity endorsements
- Charity donations
- New product line

Articles have power: They say you know your stuff and I should know because I've written a few in my time in business such as how to use twitter, the power of PR, e-networking and of course, the importance of having a business plan for your small business. The good thing about articles is that at the end you can give the 'about the author' and contact details including your direct line where people can call, email, WhatsApp you if they want to know more.

Personal PR 101: I've had over 100 media appearances including 15 on TV and do have my own personal website www.mavisamankwah.com. It's essential to register and start to develop your own personal website. After all, people are buying you first before they buy the product so why don't you give them something to work with?

Your PPRP i.e. your Personal PR Plan could include the following:

- Speaking opportunities
- Get interviewed in major press
- Have a specialist/niche area such as diversity
- Be the voice/face of your business

- Press releases targeting relevant press/media
- Imagery – Have high resolution photos on demand

In order to succeed in your PR effort you need to be consistent and have a tough skin. Call, email and never accept "No". Pretend you didn't hear and go back to them another day with something different. Most publications are always looking for new and exciting articles and what may have not been a good angle today, may be just the ticket next month so keep at it and if you have a plan, a way to execute and evaluate, you are half way there.

Wishing you BHAGs of PR success for you, your brand and for your business

MAVIS AMANKWAH

CEO of Rich Visions, Specialists in Diversity, Marketing, PR, Business & Funding Assistance

STAGE 3: REVEAL THE BRAND NEW YOU

The right cut and clarity for the best yield

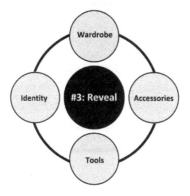

The third stage in the diamond manufacturing process involves having the diamond cut and shaped to provide the best yield, regardless of source and how much those private buyers might have paid for them. Cutting centres are all over the world from Johannesburg to Antwerp and New York. Your brand clients and competitors may be similarly spread across various geographic locations. You may sit in Chester; your client could be in Copenhagen whilst your competitor might be snapping at your heels in Charleston – thanks to the worldwide web.

When the diamonds reach their destination they are examined to decide how they are shaped and measured. Their weight in carats will then be determined – this is all regardless of source though the source may influence who buys. The quality sells the brand. That said, just like wine, some might stick to French wine only because of the source, but New World wines like Australian and South African are now leading the market. The shape and internal inclusions of the clear stone will then be marked, sawed and cleaned before going onwards to the specialist cutters who will get the gems polished and prepared for sale. Now we've unearthed our unique promise, reviewed the diamond and brought it to be developed, we still have work to do. We now have to get it to the most stylish place on earth for it to sell for the best price possible. We must also start thinking of what we would do to make your diamond sparkle continuously and this, to me, is the fun part. I'm all about fun and cannot wait to share with you what personal branding means to me. Don't get me wrong, we have to take the concept seriously, but why not have fun along the way. That's why I say it's all about serious fun!

CHAPTER 6

Your brand identity

Your logo and brand identity: Logo, typeface, tagline, tone of voice

Your logo is part of your brand just as much as your headshot is part of your brand, so don't feel that you will signpost your logo and put all your eggs into your logo doing all the work for your brand. It is very important that you spend some time and money on it for it to work hard for your business and for it to stand out, too. Long before you hire a graphic or creative designer there are some things you may have to consider. The graphic designer doesn't know what your dreams, vision and aspirations are. You have to be clear on what those are and have them written down, which we've hopefully done at stage two of our diamond mining process.

Before I bring a graphic designer into the fray, I work with my clients to create a design brief – one page only. This gives accountability from all involved and saves a lot of frustration from client to designer and everyone in between. Your design brief could contain some of the elements in the template replicated on page 60, and regardless of whether you get the work done, a good brief gives your project direction and focus. Promise me you will use one next time you have a need

Design & creative brief for

[NAME/COMPANY]

Date: DD/MM/YR

Please state clearly what your requirements are – use web-links if necessary.

This will give your design team an insight into the project so they create with **YOUR VISION** in mind.

Add other areas below as appropriate

Name(s) & contact details	
What's your business about?	
What's the unique offering?	
Which colours do you prefer/dislike and why?	
Previous project/designs	
Who is your ideal target?	
Who is your competition?	
Scope of project e.g. logo, website, social media banners	
What's the tone/feeling of the project?	
How will approvals be done and by whom?	
Provide due date(s) for project	
Budget	

for some design work. Please download a free copy from my website, www.lilymensah.com/resources, if your designer doesn't have one. A good designer should and if they don't, then you should be slightly concerned. That said, there are talented people out there who may need some structure so do not rule them out completely. If you are armed with your own design brief, the chances of things running smoothly will be increased.

In order to keep things looking consistent, it helps to have one person managing the whole process even if you decide to use multiple providers to create your brand identity. A consultant with experience takes a cohesive approach so the web designer doesn't use different colours and themes, resulting in disjointed results. Of course, not all can afford a consultant and I'm speaking from a corporate perspective, so if you want to be the project owner then do so and create a forum such as Dropbox or Google Drive so that everyone has a clear understanding of what the outcomes will be. Each person working on the project should have a copy of the design brief.

Networks online and offline

A great deal of noise has been made of online and social media in the last few years and I for one have sometimes believed the hype of it against traditional networking. Each has its own place and one cannot really live in isolation of the other. If for instance you have an online business selling clothes and everything is done online, you still have to meet people who will help you sell your stuff online or whom you could sell it to. If you have a bricks and mortar business again selling clothes, having an online presence is still essential if you are to get the most out of your enterprise and create a differentiator between you and your competitors. Moreover, people meet people often online these days before they meet in person and at the very least when they meet you and are interested in you, the first thing they do is to Google you. As I write this, I can assure you that Google is a verb and my laptop didn't have a funny green line under the word so that pretty much goes to show that you can get Googled, it's no bad thing. However if you are being Googled, what's out there about you? Does that represent the whole and complete you or sections of you that do not really add up. Having a presence that correlates both online and offline is the essence of a strong personal brand that combines the old and new effortlessly. It also shows that your brand has strong legs to travel far.

There are those times when networking can appear to be a chore, that is networking in the physical sense – this can be simply down to the fact that we are not doing it strategically and are instead applying a scattergun approach to this very important piece of armour in our arsenal of brand enhancing activities. Or we may just not know how to do it and that comes with an enormous amount of trepidation for some. We will address those quirky nuances of how to network and work the room like a pro later on in chapter 8. A quick give-away here is to always go with the intention of giving first.

CHAPTER 7

Your wardrobe – the top to toe visuals of Brand-YOU

The saying that first impressions last will never go away but I think we need to go deeper. What you wear can have a huge psychological effect on how confident you feel and the devil in this case is in the detail. I always remember my mum's advice about dressing exceptionally well on the day you are feeling poorly. Wear your best knickers AND your Sunday best. The rationale behind that is if you are suddenly taken ill to hospital and cannot speak for yourself, your clothes and especially your underwear will speak for you. If on the other hand you are wearing the grey knickers which used to be white just because they are comfortable, then the knickers might say to the emergency room professionals that you might not care too much for the body that they are about to try and save. It's common human nature to judge based on what we see. On that note I'm going to talk about the four components of our wardrobe – undergarments, clothes, shoes and other accessories.

THE UNDERGARMENTS

Just like you have a wardrobe full of clothes, I bet you there's a knicker drawer also heaving with stuff you never wear. I'm going to assume that majority of us start with our smalls and I'll explain why I've decided to dig that much deeper than is visually required.

Have you ever been sitting in a meeting and felt the underwire digging into your ribcage? I have, several times, and have then wondered why I chose that bra today, or why didn't I think through how long the day would be before reaching for the first bra out of the over-crowded knicker drawer? After suffering many of these moments, I've devised a really simple rule to make sure that I'm comfortable and there's nothing digging in.

I once heard in a movie, can't remember which, but it said that the reason why teenage girls always seemed to have long faces was because they wore thongs, and thongs by their very nature would give you a wedgie and as a result, permanent discomfort was a constant companion to them. We really do not want that, do we? I'm not saying no thongs but if you have to stay in them all day, then carefully consider whether they add to or detract from your comfort. You will be reminded of them when you should be focusing on the client or business meetings. Avoid going to the gym in thongs. If you haven't guessed, I'll explain why later.

Thankfully, I'm a huge fan of big girl pants. They cover you up really well and wedgies are uncommon so here is where we might consider sorting out your drawers – literally speaking.

Find four boxes or those wonderful folding dividers you can get from Ikea and start the separation process or shall I say segmentation process as we are doing branding here. Lightly scented paper can make it more special, too – clothes conditioner doesn't stay on for too long, does it? Now separate them into bras, knickers, slips and anything else that requires its own space, then create areas for special occasion items, everyday, smooth lines and sports.

The special occasions might be slightly lighter in volume which is good, because you don't want to spend too much time looking for said specials if time is of the essence, do you? Those specials might be lacy and racy and of multiple vibrant colours – my advice is to keep those at the back of drawer where you can see them easily though they will not be disturbed nor get easily tangled with hooks. This will ensure the delicates always look and feel delicate.

Everydays are better if they are natural and as porous in material as possible except for the bits that help with reinforcements such as waist and legs. This is something you will wear for long periods and you should look at them as the hardest working items in your wardrobe, they pull a minimum of 12-hour shifts with no coffee breaks. As such, they must feel right and support us in the best way possible or we will feel their wrath. Many underwear shops run fittings for free, and making time to grab a slot for yourself will ensure that your mammary glands will thank you for caring. Buying bras on sale just because they're half-price might be false economy because you may not use them regularly due to the fact that they cut into you or if you've lost a few pounds you don't want to be falling out of them at the wrong moment, such as picking up your bag in reception just before you shake the client's hand - do you? It's happened to a client of mine which did get to her nerves during the presentation. Her saving grace was that it was dead in the middle of winter so an overcoat saved her and she managed to escape to the ladies to 'adjust' herself.

Smooth operators have come a long way and thank goodness we don't have to wear corsets to get the right silhouette. That said, they are still important to have in your knicker drawer to keep lines and folds smooth for those days when you want to make sure that the attention is firmly on what you have to say or do rather than what your folds and lines are saying on your behalf. They also have to be comfortable and I cannot emphasise that enough. Imagine investing in smooth operators and finding that they are too tight and you are standing on stage and your windpipes are gasping for air. Personal branding as a project need not be a life-threatening affair – it should be life enhancing so please do take your time to choose a couple that fit well – try to get them on the same day as you do the bras to make the most of time and colour choices. M&S now has a great selection of smooth operators that pretty much feel like tights and do not over-hug you. They allow you to breathe. I'm sure there are other shops but my go-to place for everyday sensible knickers is M&S. Make sure it's the light control variety but you might just need the upgraded version, depending on your needs.

Sports might not be for everyone or you might just want to go for a simple jogging outfit for the odd walk in the park. Let me tell you a funny story and feel free to point and laugh, there'll be no extra charge for this. The wrong underwear can wreak havoc in your nether regions and you will want to avoid that at all costs. For instance, if you are going for a walk of 30 minutes and you get half way with the wrong underwear and have to turn back, you have to spend a gruelling 15 minutes walking in a funny way all the way home. It's happened to me and it was not funny and that I can tell you for nothing. The knock-on effect afterwards can take a while to heal too. And the less said about that, the better. So the right underwear even for getting fit makes feeling great during and after your work out all that important. Do carry a spare pair of sensible knickers to change into as thongs will do damage and leave you feeling rather bruised. Don't say I didn't warn you.

The Clothes Horse

Dress shabbily and they remember the garment; dress impeccably and they remember the woman.
Coco Chanel

I love clothes, but believe it or not, I hate shopping. How can that be, I hear you ask? Personally, I think it's the different choices that one is presented with. It can be such a really frustrating experience…shoes calling you from every window and bags just begging to be handled. Being a restless kind of person, I find that shopping represents quite a terrifying challenge for me but if I'm with a client, I find it cathartic because I know what they must be feeling like, too. Metaphorically speaking, I am standing in their shoes and they fit. If you saw me, you would think that I spend hours and hours in clothes shops up and down the country. The shocking answer is no. I've narrowed down my tastes, colours, body shape (the ever-changing one) and now focus on what I call my Fabulous F's. **F**orget **F**ashion, **F**ocus on **F**it, **F**unction, **F**lair, **F**eel and **F**abric. If you carry these F's in your pocket you are not likely to go too far out and the three things that come out as a result are 1 – save money, 2 – save time and 3 – feel fabulous and ultimately confident because you know what you love and you know what loves you back.

Body shapes are not set in stone – I have moved from pear shape to a full-ish figure as the years have gone on, so now shop for the semi-hourglass woman because finally, yes finally, I have some boobs to show – the aging process does have its advantages! I've stopped trying to shop for the shape I was

10 or 20 years ago – we change, everything changes. I used to love Liebfraumilch wine in my twenties – Blue Nun, anyone? Now we don't get on at all as my taste buds prefer the slightly dryer and fizzier variety such as Veuve. In the same way, my body is changing and my waistline has a mind of its own. Infact my waist and I do occasionally have words but hey, they are those of a friend saying, hmmm, what's going on here? Let's look at what are the general rules for most body shapes:

First of all, know your strong points and find things to flatter those assets. We all have something that we love about our bodies and that perception can also change over time – I had the perfect waist, once upon a time, for instance, and would have given the likes of Beyoncé Knowles (Mrs Carter) and Kim K a good run for their money. I still have a reasonable derriere to speak of ...oh, it's a hundred percent natural, too. If you feel it's an asset, by all means flaunt it, but be certain to know where and when.

TOP TIP

Befriend the tailor at your local dry-cleaners. They can create the perfect fit for your figure for off-the-peg clothes that don't quite fit but you like the colour and fabric.

Arms – Well toned arms are the envy of many and if you are that blessed, then show them off. A higher neckline will be more suited for that to allow you to show off your shoulders but doing both might be a tad too much – choose which to show off. The idea is to show off a little skin, but in business settings, it might be prudent to have cap-sleeves.

After a certain age however, arms on show should be done selectively and if you are presenting then covering up during the presentation is a must. We tend to have the need to be demonstrative when passionate about our subject matter and no one wants to be presented with your armpits, especially with a five o'clock shadow, or a week's worth of fuzz.

Deodorant – There is a good difference between deodorant and anti-perspirant. Deodorant just makes you smell fresh whilst antiperspirants are supposed to block and prevent the sweat glands from functioning, as they contain aluminium compounds. There are also prescription strength ones if you have something called situational sweating that can come over when you are extremely stressed, and this can be obtained over the counter at your local pharmacist. If you are prone to this, then you might want to stock the stronger stuff so that, if you are presenting, for instance, you can keep it in your tool-kit.

Presenting your QUIRKs

Boobs – If that is your blessing – I'm very envious already, but a girl cannot have everything, right? I have seen many a girl cover up with high neck featured clothes that make her boobs look like two footballs. My suggestion, to accentuate those valuable assets, is to have a lower cut neckline that separates the glands. I'm not saying so low that observers are worried and may not be able to make eye-contact. A wrap dress, illustrated further on, or something similar, does the job to yield the best cut with great results. Always remember that the more skin that is on show, the less power a woman has in the eyes of the world.

Waist – Belts could be your best friend if you have a waistline to speak of. Cinch in and they will emphasise your shape. Different colours and sizes are useful to have to enhance your outfit to match shoes, for instance. It's an area you can enhance if this fits with your shape.

Bum – These have become quite focal points for celebrities to the point that some are buying them off the shelf, literally. You can get undergarments to enhance them too. Just like a push up-bra, you can now have push-up knickers or spanks from M&S.

Clothes – Clothes make up a huge amount of our wardrobes and we tend to just buy without putting too much thought into their usefulness. The psychology attached to what we wear and how we feel is something to be mindful of before we whip out our credit cards. It refers to what it will do for us, our psyche, our confidence, our posture and of course our bank balance, which is often the last thing we think about. Just as we look in the fridge before we go shopping, it's good to look in the closet to see what we have and take stock before we step out. I recently started working with a client who happened to have a lot of the same things, mainly in green, just in varying shades and textures and the outcome of our journey was that she was not to buy anything in green for 3 months to see what she could repurpose. Harsh for many, I know but your confidence will thank you for it and so will your bank balance.

That said, we must continue to maintain good sartorial standards at all times. These do several things for us. Being well-dressed increases our confidence and we attract others to us more easily.

Shoes – No matter how tall we are, we need heels --even if they are moderate in height, they are a must in my book, especially if you are presenting or out somewhere special. I'll be the first one who will surreptitiously have a second bag with a pair of flats hidden so I can change when I get to the venue. There is no shame in that whatsoever. I'm not about to walk in the cobbled streets of London dodging potholes in order to keep my sparkle on. No way! It does pay, however, to have some heels with you so you can do the meet and greet with poise. Heels are for height so if you are blessed with height then heels may not be on your radar. However, one of my good friends, Lady Paulette, is about 5' 10" and is always in heels making her at least 6ft and above. Her argument is, and I agree with her, that heels are not just for extra height, they're for posture. Every opportunity to speak to one or more people is a networking event in my book. Shoes with heels give you that gait of refinement and improved posture.

TOP TIP

Dye shoes, if you can't find the right colour in your size

Choose sensible heels that you can comfortably stand in – two inches is more than enough and any more is a bonus. Personally, anything more than four inches will not work for me, but if you can stand in them, let alone walk in them, then bravo, go for it!

I'd also like to share a few observations about combining shoes with clothes and other accessories.

Ankle straps – As much as they do add that little bit extra, you must tread carefully about what you choose to wear with them. They have a nasty habit of being unflattering if you choose the wrong skirt or worse still, the wrong skirt length. For that reason, I avoid them if I can. That said, a bit of danger can spice things up but you must prepare in advance. Here are some tips on pulling off an ankle strap with ease:

Trousers – Wear covered toes if with trousers so only your ankle will show if you sit down and the detail will be obvious. Personally, I wouldn't combine open toes with trousers anyway. It looks slightly tacky and unpolished and more so if you haven't had time for a pedicure. This style will attract unnecessary attention to your toes.

Skirt – Should be above the knee or with a slit – this has the benefit of giving the leg added length. If the skirt is on the knee, visually, you are only showing the area between the knee and the ankle strap. The area just after your vamp and all the way to the toes is then separated, giving an illusion of shorter legs. Even leggy ladies will suffer from this too but they may not be too bothered and why should they?

The image on the next page has the illusion of nicely toned legs, and the ankle strap look brings it all together. The extra bit in the strap is the detail that will lift a rather simple dress to a different level.

Ankle strap and shoulder bag

The slit-skirt with the ankle strap – Having a suit gives a polished look but with a turtle neck, could make the look dowdy. If it's for an occasion where dowdy is required then fine, but I wouldn't put that combination together and wouldn't advise my clients to do so. It's knowing what works for your figure, and what will enhance what God has already given you that we are after here. We don't want anything to dim our sparkle, not even our choice of accessories.

The slightly more forgiving ankle strap is where you can go lower on the vamp so you get more leg – see the illustration over the page. And of course if you have a slit going high (I wouldn't go too high, though), then you have even more 'leg-room.'

A slightly more forgiving ankle strap

TOP TIP

Colours of the ankle strap should be close to skin tone or the dress to make it more forgiving. Silver or gold also work. You could have a black pair of shoes with gold straps and combine it with a black and/or gold dress for an evening do. Or just a black dress, a gold bag and accessories. Simple yet sparkling. You could also have a simple nude pair all round – depending on what nude is for your skin tone and then everyone's happy.

The wrap dress and sling-back combo – I don't know if you were looking like I was, but did you notice that that Caitlyn Jenner opted for the sling-back and wrap dress kind of look when it was time to show herself to the world? That should tell you something. I can only hazard a guess that she wanted to be still seen as powerful, yet feminine. That's my take on it – how about you? Let's look at the combo of the wrap dress and the sling-back.

These are my favourite combos of all time. I believe this is a sophisticated girl's best-kept secret. It oozes femininity and composure. It works with virtually any body shape and is forgiving – you must however have a very strong foundation (undergarments) to hold it all together. A camisole is a must and so are big-girl pants. If I hear that you've used a safety pin to hold your dress together at the bust, I'll be very, very upset. Don't do that, please. You can have your dress flared or straight depending on your shape – most of my clients go for the flared skirt with cap or 3/4 length sleeves to cover arms but leave a little skin to play with.

The choice of **sling-back** is yours. If you're dressing for a laid back affair, a peep-toe wedge is lovely and comfortable. If it's a highbrow gathering, closed toes and simple straps will take you virtually anywhere. Heels should always be shy of comfortable. What I mean is that it should allow you to stand tall with your chest out, shoulders back. My optimum heel height is 8.5 cm. Anything higher is for the party girl in me and I'd only opt for another centimetre so I can walk with some swagger in my hips. I'm sure some of you know what I mean and if you don't, ask your girlfriends about the sway of the hips and what it means to the fully feminine woman of power. Don't get me wrong, I do wear jeans and trousers but my go to is a dress or skirt suit. Check out the image overleaf on how you can do the combo with ease.

The wrap dress and sling-back combo

ACCESSORIES

Earrings & necklaces – This is when I say 'A girl CAN have too many accessories, especially when it comes to jewellery'. I will not labour the point too much however but wanted to show what I mean by that. There is one simple rule here; **the statement piece** – Choose just one for the outfit. If you choose the earring as the statement piece then the necklace should be understated or don't have one at all. If the necklace is the statement piece then a stud or something close to it is all you need. Otherwise, we are veering down the tacky and unpolished road. Or worse still we will look like we are trying too hard. It's all about the understated chic look.

Statement earrings – Absolutely perfect on their own.

Statement earring

The next combination is just a tad too much. I would keep the necklace and lose the second part of the earring if I had the option. I have a good friend who goes without earrings if she has a really bold necklace on. I'm not that bold but each to her own.

A tad too much jewellery?

Bags for your brand

> *Luxury bags make your life more pleasant, make you dream, give you confidence, and show your neighbours you're doing well.*
> **Karl Lagerfeld**

Where do I start when it comes to bags? I once read somewhere that a girl gets to an age when she develops a passion for attention-seeking handbags. I think I'm there and I now get it. Unlike shoes, they do not pinch nor do you have to worry about which height is best for which function. You don't even have to worry about your staying power in them. They just add to you and more often than not, if they attract the desired attention, they do not even have to match anything in your outfit. They can be *the* stand alone statement piece. My daughter calls them 'event' bags. Here are a couple of ways you can enhance your look with your bags:

Clutch bag – They look best if they are under your arm rather than on your waist. This will also allow you to use both hands. That said, if you want to draw attention to your hips then by all means have it there. Basically, the clutch bag, if it's a statement piece, will draw attention to the part of the body that you are carrying it on. Never on the waist, though, because we all want to have an illusion of a waist and the clutch can add inches. Below the waist is great and more comfortable for most. If under the arm, my view is the smaller the clutch the better. Because of the very nature of having to keep it close to our bodies my advice is to carry only essentials in there; one lipstick, 4 business cards, powder case with mirror, small pack of mints and if possible a phone. I'd leave keys and all other unnecessary items in the car or cloakroom.

Shoulder bag – These work really well for the slender figure. They also leave your hands free to get to business cards, pens etc, if you are at a networking event, for example. My take on these is that they should be the preserve of the taller girl (See previous image of ankle strap and shoulder bag). Especially if it's a big bag. It tends to overpower the girl with a smaller frame and we don't want a bag to outshine our unique promise, do we? It also does have, however, the added benefit of being easy to lug more heavy stuff around but be careful as it can strain your bad shoulder if you overload it, even for a day. Health and wellness also comes in, if you want your brand to have that eternal flame.

Top handles – They are definitely my favourites. Maybe because I'm on the petite side, I don't know. I however believe that this piece comes with a size and style that fits all. I've yet to meet a woman who is not in love with top-handles. If you are not in love with top-handles, inbox me on Facebook/ladymensahbrand and let's have a chat. These are so useful for the business woman, who has to keep all sorts of things in one bag and appear unruffled. It can also double up as a briefcase too if you have the right size. You can keep your business materials in there, read reports on-the-go and not feel you have to have a second bag.

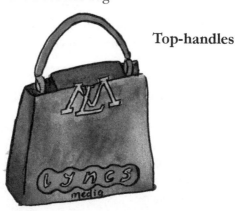

Top-handles

Another blessing is that it can go from day to evening without too much fuss. Perhaps that's why we opt for that more these days. A word of warning, though; the bigger the bag, the more inclined we are to stuff it with rubbish. Try and de-clutter weekly if you can or better still if you know you will be off to a big networking event, chuck out the receipts and flyers you don't need, for instance. This leaves room for you to dive straight into your bag if you are asked for your card. You give off the look of preparedness and being ready for business. Some good news for top-handle lovers who want a bit more. More recently, I've noticed that brands are now giving you long handles as an optional extra so look out for those when shopping if this is a requirement for you.

You could use the long strap as a belt to match the bag and that's as far as matching goes. Don't try with shoes to match. Matching shoes with a bag are no longer a requirement and thank goodness for that!

Jewellery, belts, rings and scarves are all items we can use to enhance our personal brand. And in the interest of branding and consistency, it's advisable to choose one item to stand out whilst the other accessories augment the item that we have chosen to stand out. My preference out of the above is scarves and let me share with you why I think scarves have multiple uses and can literally save a brand from complete disaster.

Do not leave home without a scarf

Actually, I believe a woman should never leave home without a scarf because they have unlimited uses outside of keeping us warm or covering our shoulders of an evening or to keep us dry from rainy days where we've been caught short without an umbrella. I have included a couple of examples for other uses below.

To enhance your outfit – a fuchsia pair of shoes may not need a bag to go with it but a mauve scarf for instance, because fuchsia is a striking and bright colour and we don't want to look like we've tried too much by getting a matching bag. Those are dated ways of looking polished and put together. My idea of style is that it should look effortlessly chic.

To save face and blushes – Have you heard the phrase, 'bump the speaker' where everyone rushes to get a word in edgeways with the speaker? Or better still speak to the speaker just before she gets on stage and then corner them afterwards. Recently, I went to an event and on the way, I just threw a scarf into my bag, even though I didn't need it for the outfit, it was just out of habit. I thought I might get cold because my body thermostat is on the blink and I go from cold to hot in less than five seconds flat. Power surges are now a constant for me so I need to have several layers to cover all eventualities. As it happened on this occasion, the room and venue were very well ventilated but the guest speaker had a major wardrobe malfunction; luckily it was just a couple of ladies and I who witnessed it. We retrieved my redundant scarf at the bottom of my bag and created a new look for her by pinning the scarf to her dress and no one batted an eye-lid – everyone thought she had changed-up a little. So, you see, carrying a scarf can save the day in more ways than one.

STRETCHING YOUR WARDROBE BUDGET

1. Find three colour combinations in your wardrobe that work well. Download a colour wheel from my website at www.lilymensah.com/resources for

suggestions but also make some up yourself. After all, it's all about you and if you don't feel like you, we are missing something here and you will not sparkle.

2. See how many outfits you can combine using the same three colours. This should include your accessories, shoes, scarves and outerwear.

3. Find complementary colours at opposite ends of the colour wheel. Just as they say opposites attract, this is no different. For example, black and white, red and blue tend to be at opposite ends of the scale and that's why they work so well together. But don't be afraid to go next door – that is called colour blocking to use the correct phrase.

Did you know that in colour theory, going from one hue to another where we pick the colour scheme of our dining room could be used here too in our wardrobe? There is some science behind it, as was first developed by Sir Isaac Newton of blessed memory. Look at the potential that you could create in your wardrobe to make Monday mornings a breeze.

Tips for getting your wardrobe colour coded

Choose three main colours that you have a lot of in your wardrobe. Mine are black/white and red. Red is the dominant colour for me and I have a series of polka dot, stripes, lace and a variety of textures but those are the main colours. I also have browns and oranges too for the cooler months. My friend and shero Rachel McGuinness (www.wakeupwithzest. com) swears by her vibrant Zesty colours and she never leaves home without her zing! She literally wears her brand colours every single day. No exception.

I have a client who did black on black so well that it was nigh on impossible to get her to change her mind about using colours until one day we went shopping together and chose colours on a trial basis so she could see the potential. It wasn't a high-end affair as we didn't want to waste money on stuff she wouldn't wear. I'm tight like that. Hate wastage in anything. We started with accessorising with more vibrant colours that she could work with. We then graduated to clothes and shoes.

Today her go-to colour in shoes is brown. This of course means if she has changed accessories, then the actual colour of the clothes will have to be updated. It's a gradual process, however.

My advice is that you don't jump in and just change because you have the funds or feel like it. Just like big brands take time to rebrand, so will your brand especially when it comes to your wardrobe. Get someone to work with you and see how you feel. A close friend who may not necessarily be a fashionista but is brutally honest might be your best bet. I have one of those. She just is too honest for me sometimes, but her honesty is what I need to keep me in check. I'm not asking you to accept judgement from those who have no business giving their opinion. Just ignore those who believe that because they are doing something one way, everyone else should be on the same page. Stay in your lane and focus on the road ahead and don't be afraid to tell others to jog on.

If you start with accessories, you are less likely to go wrong. If your hairstyle and colour have changed then a whole slew of updates will also be required in order to get the polished and understated chic look.

Use the colour wheel you have downloaded to choose how to keep them together. Bunch the themes together so reds, oranges, yellows are in that order.

Black and whites together and various shades in between. Blues and greens which should never be seen together can now be dressed up as colour-blocking.

If you have the space, do the same for your shoes, it makes the dreaded 'I have nothing to wear' be a thing of the past.

Silver jewellery should be separate from gold and pearls should be worn on their own. It's all about compartmentalising things so when you come to choose what to make you sparkle, it's so much easier and the effort of getting dressed then becomes virtually effortless.

HAIR AND MAKE-UP

I couldn't finish the body beautiful without mentioning two of a woman's most treasured features; her hair and her face. Both of them are generally fully on show when we step out. According to a report by Raconteur,[3] the UK Beauty economy alone is worth £17bn and each of us is likely to have spent over £340 in 2016 on beauty and skin care. I certainly will spend a few pounds on hair and make-up products to make sure my look is on point. How about you? If you would too, then let's have a quick overview of some basics such as hair colour, lifestyle and age.

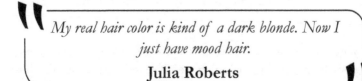

My real hair color is kind of a dark blonde. Now I just have mood hair.
Julia Roberts

Face – You may have heard the saying that once we hit forty, we should avoid keeping our natural hair colour. The rationale behind that being the texture and tones of our skin and hair start to fade with time. However, if we lighten up the hair colour a bit, then *voilà* the face also lights up. It's part of life. Getting older and wiser comes with some payback but we cannot just lie there and take it, can we? We must at least fight back. To pause or slow down some of these easily, we could start by changing our hair colour. As Julia Roberts said above, she does mood hair and I think that is such a splendid idea. Changing your hair colour according to your mood can do wonders for your self-esteem. How you frame your hair across your face should be left to a professional at least for the first few visits and if you are clever and can sort it out yourself, then go for it. I'm all for saving money and time, but it has to be done as an overall success otherwise we will end up with the wrong colour hair or cut for that big day and confidence will dip. So a word of caution is advised here.

The shape of your face will also change with time so keeping a haircut to suit your changing face will make you look current and relevant. Don't also forget to trim the hair regularly to keep it bouncy. The hairstyle you had in your twenties will not suit your lifestyle in your forties and the same goes for what you had in your thirties. Taking the plunge and going for the chop could make you look 10 years younger and the bonus is that shorter hair comes with less maintenance. My trusted associate, Sarah Houldcroft, has kindly offered her before and after photos to make the case for 'less is more' on the hair front.

courtesy of Ursula Kelly Photography

You will have to find the right hair colour for your skin tone though and DIY for the first time is still not an advisable route.

Preparing the skin for that special event

> *To be beautiful is the birthright of every woman*
> **Elizabeth Arden**

I'm certain you have your own skin care regime from masks, cleansers, serums to moisturisers. That's great but for that special event, I've found the best way to lift and plump the face quickly, is something called the oxygen facial or blast by Elizabeth Arden. I'm addicted to it! OK, my secret is out now. I have one every month or when I have a big do coming up. It's a 30-minute mini-facial and you come up feeling really pampered. The skin is cleansed and moisturised with their products, then massaged gently before the oxygen blast is used. It's essentially a light spray mixed with essential oils. It's part of their Red Door Experience. You can get one for £15 which is redeemable against any of their products so its almost as if you get it for free if you buy something from their range. To find out more, visit www.elizabetharden.co.uk/facial-services.list and let me know how you get on. My advice is to have the oxygen blast in the evening so when you can go straight home afterwards, so the products stay in place for the next day.

Make-up – An article in the *Sunday Times* magazine about a decade ago made me sit up. It was a feature on female bosses and the things they look out for and one of those things was make-up. It transpired that a large percentage of those women would think twice about hiring someone if they didn't have make-up on. Although this was a while back, I'll wager that things have not changed much for today's interviewee. A more recent article from *Marie Clare* also points to the same thing in that a bit of make-up will take you a long way in the career stakes. That's just how the land lies so it's not even worth fighting it unless you want to live as a recluse. The research is from Harvard so has to be kosher, right? I note that it's also in association with *Procter and Gamble* who has a significant market share in the beauty industry so I'm also slightly wary of the potential bias in the findings but overall, on the balance of probability, I believe there is a lot of truth in there that cannot be ignored. Here is the link for further information on make-up and your career:

www.marieclaire.com/beauty/news/a7043/makeup-affects-career-study/

TOP TIP

Get a free make-over at Bodyshop, Mac or even Superdrug but book in advance and be prepared to buy something

---

Probably the reasoning behind that is the perception that the candidate hasn't taken time to present herself, which can be likened to scuffed shoes or stained top/tie. Men on the other hand are not required to keep up with any of the above. This of course has nothing to do with whether the candidate has the skill set or not. I can understand why this would be so. My thinking is that we look our best if we put on a bit of lippy but not everyone is comfortable with lipstick. I've been known to run after my daughter begging her to put just a tiny bit on and she still refuses – she's 30. I've given up and have put it down to her experience of growing up with so much make-up around the house she's developed some sort of apathy towards it. The most I can get on her lips is Vaseline. Ugh! She does do her eyes and face though which in itself is a minor miracle. I thank the make-up artist at The Mall at Millenia in Florida, about 10 years ago, who finally got her to even consider changing her outlook.

The power of red lipstick is a phenomenon that still baffles me, though I use it to my advantage. I wear red lipstick but not every day; I choose when and where to don my coat of armour for the sassy confident lady within. It also depends on what else is going on, on my face that day. According to an article in *Psychologies*[4] magazine 'the act of applying red lipstick is empowering. By dressing your lips in red, it draws people's attention to you, especially your mouth, and subsequently, the words that come out of it.'

TOP TIP

The right shade of red could make your teeth appear whiter

We can all wear red and talk up our game without having to shout. It's getting the right shade for you that is the key. In addition, if you are going for red, you don't need the gloss. It makes its own statement. Bold, confident and powerful. Marilyn Monroe and Queen Elizabeth I both wore red with dramatic effect. Modern day icons such as Diana Ross and Beyoncé pull off red lips with such finesse. If red is not your thing yet, but you want to try it, a good department store should be your testing ground, but try it with your favourite colour clothes on so you are trying with what you already have in your wardrobe. The power and the glory of bold lips shall be yours soon enough.

Brushes, brushes, brushes! That was what I heard a lot of when I was studying in the legendary Eryka Freemantle's class as a make-up artist a couple of decades ago. Today, I still stand by that advice and say to friends and family, get good brushes, keep them clean, and application will be a near flawless affair.

Clean brushes make your make-up easier to apply. I've been known to take a client's makeup bag and empty it and chuck all her brushes in the bin. This is tough love but how can she apply her make-up well with a brush that's about 5 years old and has never been washed? Please do take this seriously, OK? Don't panic, I gave her a new set to take home and had her promise to go and get herself a second set. They need not cost the earth either. I have bought some expensive brushes in the past from professional make-up shops down London's West End, with the bag and all the fanciness that goes with being a make-up artist. Today, I get my kit from Bodyshop (www.bodyshop.com). These are really good value for money if you can time it right with an event such as their 40% off for 2 days only, you would be laughing all the way to the bank, because you got a double bargain. I'd get a set that if washed regularly can last you a few years. As long as you are alternating them, you will get real longevity out of them. Treat them like a pair of shoes. If you wear the same shoes every day, you will wear them down quickly. If you let them breathe for 24 hours with another pair, you will get more out of both shoes than if you were to stick with each day in and day out. With the brushes, I'd do a weekly wash and alternate.

Make-up and facial features – Keeping things to a minimum also goes for the face. If you go bold on the eyes, then the lips should be softer and vice versa. If you have red lipstick for that powerful statement, then the eyes should be a tad softer if not almost naked. I'm using the word naked here metaphorically. (See the illustration on the next page where the lady on the left has highlighted lips.) The best nearly-there make-up takes a whole lot longer to pull off. Reapplying and retouching to give that "Oh I've just woken up" look.

Don't be fooled, though. Nobody wakes up looking that flawless – it takes work to look immaculate, but we mustn't let others know that we've been working hard, must we? It's a game of life to present a cool exterior in order for others to feel confident in us and around us. That takes daily effort. Facebook and other social media make us all look like we lead perfect beautiful lives, and why not? We have to have an outlet to present our very best selves constantly and consistently. Personally, I work with what I have and how what is out there can fit my needs. I try not to get drawn into other people's representation of what's good on social media, because they are not me and I am not them. The mere fact that we are different means we can use what is different about us to stand out.

Smouldering, smoky eyes with nude lips – For the dramatic eyes or the smouldering, smoky look there should be very little else going on. Nude lips in a soft sheen – even gloss might be too much. Keep the drama firmly on the eyes. Cheeks should look lightly sun-kissed rather than full on rouge. More recently, contouring has been done with highlights on the top of the cheek which works really well if you don't want to have any bold colours on your face apart from the eyes. This means several applications and brushes to get the barely there look.

Highlighted Lips   **A very busy affair!**

On the other hand, if one were to add drama to the lips and face after going heavy on the eyes, then a very busy affair is presented as illustrated by the lady on the right above. Observers do not know where to look in order to focus their attention. Don't get me wrong, she looks lovely and has very prominent features that many would want to have, but, and there is a big but. There is something called 'you can do too much' and less in make-up terms is definitely more.

STAGE 4: REFINE

Refining your Brand Personality

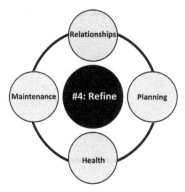

All the world's a stage

Once upon a time, manufacturers would sell cut diamonds to jewellery manufacturers who would in turn sell to wholesalers and/or retailers. The internet has changed the game slightly in that diamonds can now be sold directly with no middle man. This creates a more level playing field though it may also come with opportunities and challenges.

As the final stage of the mining process is where the stone is cut, mounted on the best metals and showcased accordingly, so too will our personal brand be brought to its final processing and refining stage. This involves several tactics such as making the best use of lighting in the shop window, hiring the best sales people, location, marketing, promotion and what have you.

Once that diamond is bought, it also needs to be kept secure, insured even and polished regularly in order to keep it as beautiful as the day it was first mounted.

Of course, the final stage also means that your diamond will be on show for all to see and why not? We are here to work our QUIRKS. No one will see the diamond if it is hidden in the glorious box at the bottom of your jewellery case only for special occasions. I say, every day is special and your beautiful diamond shouldn't be hidden from the world. Show it, show up, work your personality and let it be the indelible ink that runs through everything that represents your brand.

CHAPTER 8

Keeping the diamond sparkling from all shop windows

In this chapter we are going to look at:

◊ Networking and your brand promise

◊ Abundance & circles of influence

◊ LinkedIn - The perfect setting

◊ Other networks and your brand online

NETWORKING AND YOUR BRAND PROMISE

Showing up at events and being present

Networking is that space where we give with an attitude and mind-set that will yield its own results in often unexpected ways.

Many years ago, if you had said that I could walk into a room by myself in the name of networking and speak to complete strangers, I would have gulped with abject fear...the kind of fear that cripples you and makes you want to run away, but you are glued to the floor. The kind that you see in your dreams when you try to wake up and cannot move. Yes, that kind of fear. But being an entrepreneur brings out the do or die attitude because it takes getting out of our comfort zone in order to make things happen. My argument is that if we stay in our fear zone we'll soon be obsolete anyway, so best to get out and do it and see what happens. That's exactly what I did. More so for me it was one of these networking events full of grey suits and stuffy blokes. I didn't dare think much about it before hand. I was up on a bleak Thursday morning and had paid in advance so off I took myself to meet new people. Luckily for me it wasn't so bad and being one of a slightly different shade and sex, I stood out like a sore thumb – that was my QUIRK! It was my difference that made it for me and I embraced it in a second. People wanted to know who this new kid was that had dared to enter their realm with such aplomb! Again, being a bit quirky does have its benefits, you stand out without even trying and to top it, I wore the brightest smile you can ever imagine. The rest is of course history as (1) I didn't die and (2), I made great mutually beneficial contacts that are still around today.

Where to network

This is a million dollar question for most, including me. The answer is; where are your potential clients? If they hang out at restaurants on a Friday night, that's where you'd want to be. Your network should be profiled around them rather than just where you enjoy hanging out. It's part of your business development programme; always be prepared because you don't know where the next big gig is going to come from.

Remember also, that as a business owner, you are on call all the time - junior doctor hours have nothing on those of the entrepreneur, because the buck really does stop with you. Your name is on the door of your business and therefore you are forever wedded to your business, in a sense.

Find partnerships and collaborators

There are times that business will be so busy, yes, it does happen that you cannot cope with everything by yourself and that's when you should have a bank of people you can call upon to provide assistance, help, whatever you want to call it but it shouldn't be done on the hoof. These are people you would have had in your proverbial Filofax for a while and they may be able to drop everything for you. (See the Circles of Influence illustration on page 110, particularly the Exclusive Circle.)

Increase reach of those people centred events.

If you are doing a lot of your networking online you might want to make it more offline – even if by phone. Touching base with people every now and again will be useful for the longer term – you don't have to be physically present. Video is one area we will look at in a bit more detail in the Brand Make-over Essentials later on in chapter 9.

Increasing your client base by 20% or 50% will not happen in a vacuum and especially if you are selling people centred products or services, then you have to sell your why to those who may want to know about you. Not just the target audience mentioned earlier but those who know them and might pass it on. Sell the reason why you do what you do.

Your personal brand statement

Some call it the elevator speech, but as we are talking about brand promise this section will help you craft a winning personal brand statement that you can update according to where you find yourself. It should be something that either your mum or kids or your gobby 13-year old niece will understand. Leave fancy words out – most people will switch off.

At networking events, we are often asked by the savvy networker "Tell me, what do you do?" That's when some of us freeze. Well, I used to and there's no shame in admitting that I was once petrified to speak about myself and my services until I crafted a 45 second personal brand statement. You can do the same so you always have it in your back pocket and can recite it at will. Use this layout to help you craft our own:

- Your name
- Your position
- Your company
- Your location
- Up to 3 main areas of what you do
- Benefits
- Outcome
- Finish with your name, company and catchphrase

Here is mine:

"My name is Lily Mensah, brand ambassador of Lyncs Media based in London. We work with business women around the world to make them look fabulous on paper, online and in person. This involves their business cards, online profile such as LinkedIn, and their professional wardrobe. This increases their visibility and their personal brand. If you know someone who might benefit from my service, pass on my details and tell them to let me know that you sent them. Again, my name is Lily Mensah, brand ambassador of Lyncs Media and my job is to make your brand sparkle."

I have mine on my phone and do recite it often before an event. Preparedness makes your brand sparkle, effortlessly.

Carry your business cards

The wallet is the best place to keep them handy because that's where you keep your credit cards and cash and you never leave home without them, do you? A handful is plenty. As your business cards will also have a QR Code (Quick Response Code) on them, keep the last one and ask the person you have just met to scan the QR code on your card because you would have created it with all your contact details on them. QR codes give your brand collagen or an oxygen facial. Get one and give your brand instant Botox! Here's my QR code so you can scan and get my contact details right here.

What should be on your QR code?

- Name,
- Website
- Phone number
- Any other relevant contact details, including your online and social media handles.

Use the text version as it gives you more flexibility. I got mine free at www.the-qrcode-generator.com/

What are the benefits of a QR code apart from giving information?

For me it's current and trendy and it makes me look 20 years younger, like I'm down with the kids. Well, almost. A couple of years ago, I met an intern at a networking event and I had worked the room quite well. Consequently, I had run out of cards. This young woman started speaking to me about job opportunities and branding to be more visible. I was down to my last card so I asked her to scan the QR code onto her phone. The look of respect on her face was a picture after my contact details were revealed. It said something like, how can a woman of a certain age be so current?

Diversify your network

In the networking game, it's easy to keep to the same networks because they are familiar and you know what you get. However, how long will those networks around people you know such as friends and family fulfil your respective needs and then expire? There are some that will recommend keeping to the same network and whilst that has a place for those who are niching exclusively in a particular industry, it pays to extend your reach that little bit further. It's refreshing too just so you get out your funk a little. Having that butterfly in your belly means you are always testing new places and people and having different conversations. Even to the point of learning new tricks to keep your brand relevant.

It's very tempting to keep with the people you know or came with because it feels comfortable. I have to remind myself that when I go networking, I want to meet new people so the person I'm with is not going to take up too much of my time when there. Of course you can regroup later on your way home but it defeats the object of networking when you stay with your friends or colleagues. Why bother going at all – you might as well have stopped at the coffee shop or wine bar instead. It pays to set your goal for a particular networking event too. You could decide that you'd like to meet a certain type of person – why don't you ask your host to introduce you if there is one such person. The going for the sake of going makes it difficult to review whether your efforts are worthwhile.

TIPS FOR SUCCESSFUL NETWORKING

Business cards - have cards, preferably in a holder, making it accessible, not under your umbrella in an oversized handbag.

Take it out of your bag if you can and if you have a pocket, even better, but us women, we tend not to have clothes with numerous pockets therefore may not always have easy access but recommended.

Name tags

Do your own – you can get one from Amazon for about £10. Get the tags with magnetic fixings to protect the more delicate materials like silk. You don't want to be one of many where your badge will say Hello..... My name is...... Do you? As much as I love event organisers who do the most difficult jobs of making sure everyone is happy, they cannot just sort out individual personalised tags, and why should they? You should absolutely invest in your own name tag, own it and stand out! One 'meet & greet' lady at an event said to me –"Oh, our badges not good enough for you then?" I replied, "On the contrary, yours is just fine, I'm just very fond of my own, that's all."

Some might prefer the company name first but my suggestion is to have your name first, position second and company name last. This is how you would introduce yourself in your personal brand statement so having a similar approach on your written branding material makes you more memorable. After all, we are buying you first, before the company and that has always been my approach.

Mobile phone etiquette

Yonks ago, I might have gone as far as saying no mobile phones but I guess in today's world we use it more for photos, contacts and social media. Avoid answering it if it rings, though, unless it's an emergency. I often have mine in my bag and only have my cards with me. If I need to get the phone, I reach into my bag for it and wait towards the end of the event, when I've gelled with a lot more people before taking photos. I do like the photo opportunity – it also reminds me of who was there and what we talked about. I occasionally send photos as a follow-up. It's the preserve of women to take photos of themselves.

Video and show-reels are also a good way of reconnecting all the women you've met during the meeting by posting on Facebook as a reminder. If under a minute, Instagram it and tag all the ladies, everyone wins. Don't overdo it, though, as it starts to get annoying. I save the show-reels for big events and try and only add the good pictures, not when someone has just taken a mouthful of spinach and their teeth are green – you know what I mean. If you show people in the right light, you become a trusted photo-taker so they are more willing to pose next time. I have been known to send to men too, but not very often as (1) they tend to be camera shy and (2), it might send the wrong message.

Mind your own brand and listen up!

> *Always listen! Interestingly the word listen and silent have the same letters!*
> **Stella Fehmi**

The funny thing is that in minding your own brand you will have to be more attentive towards others. This supports you in that you get to understand what their needs are and by so doing, you are able to help personally or recommend someone else. It also allows you to introduce others when they meet. I'm terrible at names but my often saving grace is people's family – I always like to see if the person shares some of my family interests – for instance. I'm at an age where my kids are adults in the eyes of the law and I'm also lucky enough to have a young-minded 81-year-old mother so that combination keeps me pretty busy. I'm told I'm one of numerous people who have become the 'sandwich generation' so if I'm not talking about exams and finding career interest for young adults, I'm discussing how best to find that balance to see Mum as often as I can. Many a business woman I know has one or both challenges/blessings depending on your outlook of the day. That in itself is an ice-breaker. Oh and when you get the grandkids stories, the discussions get that much richer. How else can we give of our knowledge and expertise to our network if we are not there to listen but to just sell and hand out cards? There is a way and a trick to it.

Listening more than you speak takes a lot of skill and as my mum would always remind me, God didn't give you two ears and one mouth for nothing, so listen more and talk less. As much as I don't always get it right, I try to listen as much as I can. That is networking 101 and the bonus is that listening allows you to know a bit more about the person you are speaking with in order to introduce them to a third person.

Following are some more networking tips and tricks from another one of my sheroes, Stella Fehmi, a powerhouse when it comes to the subject of meet and greet and she always does it with a dazzling smile.

Stella Fehmi – Networking tips and tricks

It is estimated that 97% of self-employed people rely on contacts and referrals to get work. This shows the importance of Networks.

Francis Kay, Brilliant Business connections

If you pick up a dictionary and look up 'network' this is what it says: people connected by the exchange of information professionally or socially. So, in business terms networking describes the giving and taking process of exchanging leads, contacts, recommendations, business strategy ideas and other information, through established groups or relationships, with the aim of making business easier and ultimately more profitable.

Being involved and really using the networking circuit – is an ART! Yes, Networking is an art – it's the art of knowing how to make good use of friendships, social settings, business forums and gatherings; in fact, any situation that brings people together to sell themselves and, as a result their products and services.

Networking is very much "any place, anytime, anywhere!" And it's massively more about your ATTITUDE and strategy or tactics. You need to start by thinking and identifying what you hope/want to gain from your networking process. Do you want to generate more sales? Raise your business profile? Raise your company's profile or gain information and support? Your networking should be seen as an investment for the future. Things might be OK now, but in harder times, when business is quieter, it could be your professional network that carries you through. Harvey MacKay, successful businessman and author, explains this nicely as "digging your well before you get thirsty"

Five Reasons why women are GREAT at networking

Women have been doing 'it' from time immemorial; networking that is! So practice makes perfect and here are just a few points, which I'm sure you will all know, about why we are so good at it.

Yes, yes, yes – we've heard it all before – all the jokes about gossiping. But do you know that when it comes to networking WE WOMEN have a definite, scientific advantage. "What?" I hear you say. Well, it starts with BIOLOGY, which takes us to the first point:

1. Hormones. (No not those ones) OXYITOCIN – known as the "bonding hormone" allowing us to incorporate the trust and empathy in groups – great for NETWORKING!

2. Empathy. As women, we know and understand that networking boosts our confidence and gives us a sense of pride. So, often many ladies have said how empowered and validated they feel when networking at meetings and events.

3. Lifelong Learning. Women realise the educational benefits of networking and are more likely to learn one new tip or a golden nugget of information to take away and implement in their own businesses. Having the opportunity to brainstorm with others really can save you time and money.

4. Professionalism. As women we understand how networking can improve our credentials and professional standing in the business circles. The more serious you are about investing time into your business, the more serious others will be about your business!

5. More Business with the Feminine Touch. It goes without saying how women understand the power of networking which leads to new business and contacts. So, many times we hear how a new business

connection has led to clients, sales, investors and other important contacts.

Manage your mood – top tip! When you stay positive, you will always be able to do more, give more and ultimately have a successful day.

Tips and tricks of networking

Think about how you make someone feel – the most successful networkers are good at making other people feel special. Every month make an effort to give away at least five business cards you've received to other connections outside your network (with permission of course). If you can help someone else secure new business through your referral it's a win-win.

Make sure you are an active networker - that's the key.... don't know what an active networker looks like? You will have to contact me for that ha ha!

Networking definitely widens your circle of influence. Due to the number of years I have been in the game, I now have a wide network and because of this I was recently indicated as one of LinkedIn's top 1% of influencers on the now 400 million global online networking social media site. I, along with other Athena Network Regional Director's own and manage a LinkedIn Group for members and others. Not to mention the circles on Twitter and Facebook! So, from a personal perspective, I hope you can see why networking is so important for you and your business!

Think about how you stand to profit from networking. Ultimately it is a vehicle we use for sales, developed through the relationships we create with other people. Networking functions and events provide the opportunity for us to expand our contact list and begin the process of know, like and trust for mutual business or potential business leads. Focus on quality contacts over quantity and make a positive first impression.

Being visible and getting noticed is a big benefit of networking. Make sure you regularly attend business and social events that will help to get your face known. You can then help to build your reputation as a knowledgeable, reliable and supportive person by offering useful information or tips to people who need it. You are also more likely to get leads and referrals as you will be the one that pops into their head when they need what you offer.

The people that you hang around with and talk to do influence who you are and what you do, so it is important to surround yourself with positive, uplifting people that help you to grow and thrive as a business owner. I really love helping other people, and networking is a fantastic way that allows me to do this easily. Networking is full of business owners that have problems or issues within their business that need solving, and there is great satisfaction in helping someone to solve a problem they have and get a fantastic result from it.

Success is in the follow up - this is where the real work begins! Follow up sooner rather than later. Show you are interested and arrange to connect further.

Angela Mayo's quote resonates very strongly with me:

> *"I've learned that people will forget what you said, people will forget what you did, but people will never forget how you made them feel."*

That's my secret - *The Mayo Effect*

Friendships form through networking

Lastly, this tip is more personal than business related, but is a big benefit nonetheless. Many friendships form as a result of networking. Personally, I have achieved so much with the opportunities presented to me through networking such as my partnership in *Businessworx* and being on the front cover of Global Woman magazine.

Stella Fehmi, Networking Supremo, Athena Network West Essex & City Regions

CHAPTER 8

ABUNDANCE & CIRCLES OF INFLUENCE

> *"Lots of people want to ride with you in the limo, but what you want is someone who will take the bus with you when the limo breaks down."*
> **Oprah Winfrey**

Today things have changed with the Internet and social media. I've had to get out of my comfort zone yet again in order to make myself more interesting and memorable. The most useful advice I've been given in networking is that one must have a mind-set of abundance. There will always be enough food for all of us if we share what we have on our plate. A collaborative mind-set ensures that those that come our way will have been attracted by our abundance of spirit. It also attracts those who recognise the spirit with which we present ourselves and ideas.

There will be times when you will be seen as a source of free information. Give anyway, because in life there will be those who come to you for various reasons. Some, we will have to give freely to, some will come already prepared to buy, and some will come looking for that exclusivity. Through those encounters we learn to create incremental circles of influence with varying levels of connectivity, which I call the four circles of influence. These are the outer circle, inner circle, exclusive circle and finally the circle of sheroes. Benefits of the circles are arranged around the 80/20 Pareto principle. A principle that suggests that 80% of outcomes come from 20% of our overall effort so for instance 20% of your clients may bring 80% of your overall revenue. Let's review the circles of influence further.

Circles of influence

BRAND YOU

Outer circle

They are those you meet fleetingly but have some sort of connection with; for example, your online connections you hardly engage with but are there regardless. We all have them. These are also people you meet at networking events or those you worked with or went to school with that you have an affinity with. Their circle value will probably be up to 20/80 with neither party gaining much, if anything.

Inner circle

Acquaintances that you connect with regularly at networking events and you have their number but never really use it. They are on your database and you are on theirs. The type of relationship is reciprocal and knowledge and opportunities may occasionally be exchanged. You spend some time with them, but infrequently. Their circle of value will therefore be around the 40/60 mark and you may buy from them or support a cause of theirs and vice versa. You share common or similar ideals and values.

Exclusive circle

These will be members of a close community of business and personal relationships that go beyond the 9-5. You might be on first name terms with some of their family members. They actively look out for you and bring real opportunities rather than just the odd Christmas card and a hello. They don't just "like" on social media, they comment and share. There is commitment from both parties and an unspoken acceptance that you will have their back. If there is a last minute glitch, for example, you can call them and they will be there. If they can't help, they send you someone else who can. That quiet confidence in one another is there and they also know that you will do the same for them. Those are the ones that bring the most and of course they will be fewer in number. Their circle of value is closer to the 60/40 mark, if not more.

Sheroes

These are the women you can count on for everything. Business is not just about how to balance the balance sheet. It's about having a balanced lifestyle and these women and sometimes men will do so too with you. They are the sheroes. I have a few in my mental Filofax. As I was writing this book, one shero I've known for more decades than I care to remember, Ms Kiki, would beg me to finish my word quota of the day when all I wanted to do was go out and hang out or sleep on a Sunday afternoon. Their circle of value is – 80/20. They bring food if you are not up to it. They bring soul and spiritual food, too, not just bread to break. These are "goal-friends" as my mentor and coach, William Arruda, calls them. I have never sought money from them and they have never done otherwise. But I bet if I was down to my last dollar with a good reason to go with a begging bowl, I'm sure they will provide knowing that I will keep to my word and pay back. There will be no questions asked. This is where we should all aim to be but then as we know, not everyone can fit in to the shero circle and it takes years to build.

THE PERFECT SETTING FOR YOUR PROFESSIONAL BRAND ONLINE

There are a few professional business network platforms that can really bring your 'sparkle' out and are the perfect setting for your personal brand. My favourite is LinkedIn so I am going to give you the low-down on how to use this network effectively.

LinkedIn

Fact – there are fewer women on LinkedIn than men. Fact – fewer women are active on LinkedIn than men. Give us Facebook or Instagram and we are there with our clicks, likes, comments and replies. My mission here is to get more of us involved and active on LinkedIn because guess what? It's one of the first places that come up if you are Googled, and it better say something nice and engaging. Don't you think?

Why am I so passionate about LinkedIn, you might ask? You see as business women, we are also professionals and as much as we have the best gigs and products in town, people still want to know if we have the expertise to do what we say we can do and the go to place is LinkedIn. It is estimated that there are 106 million users[5] who visit the site each month and 40% of users check in daily. So if we are not showcasing our best selves on there, we are missing out on lots of opportunities to shine and get seen and ultimately do more business. A business contact told me that LinkedIn is like the IOD (Institute of Directors) of social media; full of stuffy blokes in dark suits. Well, if we want to join the IOD and break down those social barriers we have to weigh in not sit by the side-lines watching and gawping.

CHAPTER 8

What are the benefits?

500+ is the magic number that on LinkedIn appears against anyone with over 500 connections regardless of whether you have 501 or 5000. This is used as a visual and psychological yardstick for a person's connectedness. Don't ask me why but what I know for sure is that if you have over 500+, people seem to think that you have cultivated enough value on your professional brand. I often say to my clients, get known by getting 500+. Again, there are more men with the magic number than there are women. My question to most of us women is, why are we so hesitant in showing our faces and flexing our professional muscles?

If we don't flex then few, including our fellow businesswomen will see our unique value. And it is such a joy for me to see more women commenting on posts instead of worrying about whether we will be judged by what we do say and if what we do add is of value or not. It's the social equivalent of the imposter syndrome which psychologists Dr. Pauline R. Clance and Suzanne A. Imes have written about so I will not labour over it here. The sad thing is that this is often limited to high achievers and it pains me to see really talented women shy away from showcasing their expertise in case they offend. Tsk! If it makes sense to you, then it's OK. Let's comment, share and celebrate our successes online on the world's largest professional network.

To accept or not to accept

There's always a question as to who to accept and again, we tend not to because we don't know them. If you are the cautious type, I completely understand. Why not have a look at their profile first and accept anyway. If they immediately follow it with a long salesy email, then you know what to do. DELETE! It's unlikely to create a problem as this is a professional platform and stalking is very much frowned upon so don't be shy. You just never know who they might know that could be of mutual benefit. Do always remember the quote about everyone having 6 degrees of separation from the person they wish to connect with – LinkedIn narrows it somewhat to 2 to 3 degrees.

Organise your content for maximum value

There are no real hard and fast rules about how to organise your content but as a trainer on the subject, my advice on the main areas that you should focus on in order to get extra mileage on your personal brand are Headshot, Headline and Summary. Let's look at these three in more detail.

Headshot – Every profile must have one. Personally, if you don't have a headshot, I will hesitate to accept an invite from you, unless I know you well where I'll accept and then send you a private message to get it sorted out sharpish. Many will not even engage with you at all and that's the power of a photograph. So what makes a good photograph you might ask? Just remember the 4 simple rules of engagement for this. 1. It says a headshot so it should be above the chest, closer to your shoulder. 2. Jewellery should be minimal. 3. Look slightly away from the camera – won't tell you off for looking at the camera though, we just don't want to be seen to be staring down at people when they click on our profiles and 4. Keep it current.

Remember LinkedIn can look a bit like a dating site for professionals. If you put a photo of you that was taken 10 years ago and you were looking young with a full head of hair then make sure that you still do today. If you've had a hairstyle change for instance – then it's time to do an update of the photo too.

CHAPTER 8

A few months ago, I decided to change my look slightly for a couple of months, and I bumped into a lady I had been speaking to remotely. I was very nervous about meeting her because that was the first time we had met face to face. My first question was, "Do you recognise me?" Thankfully she said yes, but then went on to add that even though my hair was longer, my face was still the same so it was easy to spot me. Phew! She then added that some people are not so lucky and she's been known to walk into a restaurant looking for someone when they were right in front of them just because they don't look anything like their photo. So let's keep our profile picture current to avoid brand confusion at best.

How much face do you show on the picture? Please do not stand too far back. The optimum is 80% of your face should be in the headshot. We want to see your face not a picture of you standing by the beach in your sunglasses. Unless you wear eyeglasses all the time, you should not wear them in your headshot. It's non-negotiable. Why? Because people who don't know you may only be able to make a quick judgement call on your profile picture and decide there and then whether you are trustworthy or not. As much as you want to look cool and relaxed, LinkedIn is not the place for coolness. Instagram and Facebook are cool places to showcase your sunnies.

I've been asked, "How can I get a professional photo done if I don't know photographer?" Well, there are many photo shops on the high street and my best one is Snappy Snaps. They'll do a good set for you for around £40 investment. You can use this on your other social media site, website etc. so don't scrimp too much when it comes to your headshot. Below are the dimensions from the LinkedIn website.

File size - 10MB maximum,
Your photo should be square.

The ideal pixel size for your photo is 400 x 400. If either width or height exceeds 20,000 pixels, your photo will not upload.

Headline – This is 120 characters only. Use it. You have just this amount of characters to tell people about your professional prowess so it's imperative that you use it wisely. If you don't, LinkedIn will default to your current position. I always say you are worth more than your job description. If you have a specialty, showcase it, a niche delivery of services, that's all fine. A winning headline for a coach for middle management women in financial services should have experience – accolades – services – outcomes rather than just the job-title.

Summary – This is exactly 2000 characters. This is not where you dump your CV. Stop that already! We want to know about you therefore you have the opportunity to tell the world who you are, what you do, why they should care. Don't forget to add slight warm and fuzzy stuff and finally a call to action. Simple, right? You would have thought so. The best wordsmiths get stuck in their tracks when it comes to writing this bit about themselves so don't beat yourself up too much if you do. It's about knowing what the simple rules are about what to use and how much is too much. I've seen many who just put bullet points and left it at that, but we are building a brand worthy of note so let's stretch and flex our brand muscles here, too.

I tend to do this in a few ways. Below is a template you might want to follow:

◊ Keywords about you and industry. If you have done your initial research in chapter 2 about what makes you unique then you should have loads of keywords to play with. For instance, if you have been described as motivational and energetic, use those words. Colourful and fun if the industry allows it. Creative and diverse, and talented are all inviting words that you could use in your opening paragraph about you. If you have industry buzzwords, there's no reason why you can't borrow from them, so your profile is aligned with what people will be looking for on the platform.

◊ Why you do what you do? You should have a "why" so people know that there is some passion behind the credentials that you have. This opens up the conversation when those who might not know you, start to have a chat with you or even send a message. Of course there might be some who will spam you but that's a small price we have to pay for social media. Don't forget to include the people or professionals you want to work with.

◊ 3 main areas of focus. As tempting as it is to put all your skills in there, try and narrow down to just three for the purposes of this exercise so people are clearer in having a conversation around those specialties. Other activities that you do will be evident once you start doing more posting, commenting and writing articles. LinkedIn is not supposed to be a static platform, so if you have a change of focus or direction, you have the option of updating your profile too. I have a client who is a speaker, coach and author. That means she describes those three areas directly with a couple of lines to spare.

◊ Extra-curricular activity and values. We've often been told that showing the warm and fuzzy side in a professional setting is taboo. I say boo to that! It isn't. We are human beings first and if we start with our own humanity, then the likelihood is that those who choose to do business with us will get a flavour of other aspects of our personalities. You will never please everyone, so let those we work with, or have the opportunity to speak with, know in advance where we stand, including our values.

◊ Call to action. Very important – let people know what and why they might want to contact you. Email is always at the top of your profile, underneath your headshot, but because it is not always obvious, it helps to have it available if you have space to do so. If not, let people know how to find you with a link at the end of your summary.

Publish articles

Articles are such great brand enhancing vehicles and as much as it takes time to craft one, they are never a waste of time. It helps cultivate trust in your brand. I'm absolutely delighted now that we mortals are allowed to publish on the platform at all, even if we are used as warm-up acts for Influencers. It still gives us an opportunity to tell people what we are passionate about and how we can help them. The bonus there is that you get to brag a little about you, so don't forget to craft an "about the author" in your posts. More opportunities to sparkle!

Join groups

Not too long ago, one could only join 50 groups but now that cap has been expanded. I have quite a few but have often tried to keep it to under 50 and have deleted the not so active ones. In joining groups there are a few things to be aware of, and in this case size doesn't always win. It's about the activity that exists within the groups. There could be a group of over 1000 members that has hardly had any posts or discussion in the last month, for instance. This is not a good way to use your group numbers. There could be a group of about 250 members who are very active and it's worth trying to join a broad selection and don't just be a spectator. Your visibility involves you getting involved. Start by liking, then commenting to get a feel for how they operate. Then jump in by sharing your posts. You do not have to be the original creator of the content -- if you are seen as a sharer, then you will be trusted as a carer too. More so, if you see a post by another woman, and you like it, share it so this encourages more of us to make the time to share our expertise – don't just read and move on. In commenting and liking, we are helping other women shine as the more engagement of posts one gets on the platform, the more their profile stands out. This is all part of my mission to get more female brands sparkling with minimum effort.

Recommendations

These are GOLD on this platform. If someone does something for you, thank them via LinkedIn, openly if it's to do with business. These are set out in such a way that it's one of the first things you see and on page 1 of your profile unless of course you have reorganised it in a way that makes room for more content upfront. It goes a really long way as those looking on undercover might glean a lot more about your professional prowess if you have a few recommendations. There are those who say more is better but I disagree. What is important is that the person making the recommendation and what they say is relevant to your current business. Do not hesitate though to ask for recommendations either. If you don't ask, you don't get. I know we are all busy but most do get around to doing the recommendation – the well intentioned ones, that is. I've been known to do a recommendation 4 months after being asked. Not perfect, but at least I did it. I have also received recommendations months after the event. If you craft something for them, it might make it slightly easy, but I know this is not encouraged by the powers that be at LI headquarters. Ah, well – can't win them all, can we.

Daily Check-in

Ten minutes is all you need to keep the brand building activity alive, and if you have a long commute this is the perfect opportunity to do so. The algorithm is such that the more you check in; the more it lifts your profile, so you have to feed it something on a daily basis. It's very easy to do so if you have the app on your phone. Say congrats, happy birthday or just send a message to say "Hi, how are you doing". This provides the high touch to the socially remote world that we live in and keeps your contacts reminded of your brand and vice versa.

Personalised invitation on-the-go

You may wonder how to do this without being behind a computer. This may change in time as LinkedIn has a habit of moving things around without telling anyone, but for now this is what I know and can share with you. Look at the three dots to the top right hand side of the picture below:

When you click on that you get the following options and choose 'Personalize invite'

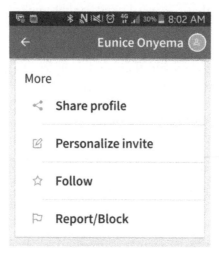

Anyway, you get to say 'Hi' properly as you can see below from the screenshot. It's that simple so please do not send the standard 'Hi Eunice, I'd like to add you to my professional network'.

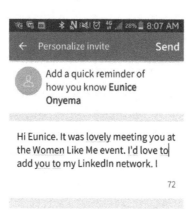

Unless you know the person well and they are expecting an invite, it helps to give it a certain level of personalisation so for instance if you met someone at a networking event, say so and see how quickly the invite will come back with an acceptance. If you haven't met them, their credentials or other activity that they are linked to that might be of interest. You can tap into that. At the very minimum, if they have published an article or shared something of value and you like the post, say so and that is a lovely way to give someone a subtle endorsement of their work.

Other professional websites

BeBee: www.bebee.com
Other professional websites are springing up and at the moment BeBee seems to be gaining ground. They are mixing business with pleasure and the idea is that more and more people just don't want to have that static professional life and people tend to now want to mix the two. For instance you might want to find a beautician who likes to hike in her free time. That's where you will find BeBee's value.

Brandyourself: www.Brandyourself.com
This website and all its tools will allow you to monitor and manage what's shown about you in Google. Please note that it will not do personal branding for you. You have to feed it information and you have to provide the relevant links that work for your brand. The optimum is to have the first 10 items of a Google search about you and for that to happen, you have to be active on many feeds, social networking sites, blogs and so on. It's what you feed the Internet about you that shows up and in case there is information that is not relevant to you, you have the opportunity to delete or hide the information yourself.

AboutMe: www.about.me
You have the opportunity to tell your story in your own unique way.

I once heard someone say that there are now apps for personal branding. Really? The thing is that apps are tools which help and make the outcomes easier to achieve but they are still just tools. Look at them as someone giving you a mower for your garden. It is just a tool. You either mow it yourself or get a professional to do it for you. As much as the mower will not mow the lawn by itself and is a lot better than doing the lawn with a cutlass, neither will the apps create a brand for you, they will just make the process easier, and human intervention is almost always required to make the work stand out.

Social networks alone will not cut the ice. Human beings need to be seen in the flesh; it's that innate need to have intimacy that leads to trust. The increase in use of video (we will be looking at this in more detail in chapter 9) is closing that gap in social media and the high-tech world of business because you are more realistic in video than in a static photo. And video is getting bigger and bigger, but be warned. There is a limit to how much people can stand looking at or listening to you. According to research it is a minute to 90 seconds and we move on to other things. Constantly bombarding people with your show-reel on a daily basis will alienate followers because they are investing their time in you, so let's not over-do it, please. We cannot take for granted that they will continue to view when really relevant information is at hand. If you have built some sort of trust, we need to manage it carefully and sensibly. Having a campaign of being there all the time versus being there when relevant may be the difference between how your brand promise will be valued online.

CHAPTER 9

Maintaining the dazzle in Brand-YOU

It's all very well having a beautiful sparkling diamond but if you don't look after it and polish it from time to time it will lose its lustre. Exactly the same goes for your brand; if you don't maintain it, look after it, you will find it loses its sparkle and effectiveness. So in this chapter we are going to make sure you are not going to let your shining gem become dull and uninteresting.

Just like the many facets of a diamond there are lots of ways to keep Brand-YOU sparkling. So let's get polishing.

Relationship management

Once upon a time, when 5p.m. came, we left work and dismissed all thoughts of our colleagues until we encountered them at the coffee machine or photocopier the following morning. How different it is today, when we have 24/7, 365 day access not only to our close contacts but to many other folks from all walks of life, some of whom we've never met and indeed may never shake hands with in person. Our relationships are no longer restricted to the boardroom, the wine bar or the nineteenth hole at the golf course. So how do we apply the art of old school relationship management to today's world where we are always on call?

Ask not what your network can do for you! GIVE.

Those who have been in the relationship management game for a while are aware that the number one rule of networking is to GIVE.

Improving long distance relationships

How can we be more visible and endearing within our network, since an online presence only goes so far? The last time I checked, the telephone was still an acceptable mode of communication, so why aren't we using it more? Modern technology has made it easier and more cost-effective than ever to mix the old with the new when connecting with our global contacts. How about occasionally forgoing the text and emailing but create Skype, Facetime or Hangout moments? Those non-verbal cues do make the dialogue that much richer. The personal touch of a phone call might be the only differentiator that sets your brand apart from the dullness and monotony of email and/or text.

The size of our database shouldn't define us.

At one time, we knew people either by their first, last, or occasionally their nicknames. Now it's by their @handle or username. I get it. It's a sign of the times we live in. According to Pew Research[6] the average Facebook user has 238 friends. LinkedIn's magic number is 500+. A person's name is (to them) the sweetest and most important sound in any language. So using only handle and usernames to win friends and influence people is surely not going to cut it, is it? If you hear someone boast about the number of online friends or contacts, ask them if they know the real names of all these contacts…or better still, if they know the name of just one person's child or pet. That should settle it, I think.

All said and done, one fundamental component of your personal brand cannot be ignored: Only you can do you - you own the intellectual property.

Your online presence

Who is checking you out? You will never quite know who has checked you out and what is out there about you, so it makes sense that all that you have out there is relevant to your brand and doesn't take away from it. Being in business means we often have to mix business with pleasure. As much as you would like to have your private and personal separate from your business and professional, I think that is no longer possible. Everything is out there in the open. Some go as far as uploading the dinner they had last night but each to his (or her) own – I am not God so I cannot not judge but I wouldn't do so myself and if you are my client I'd recommend that my clients do not engage in such activity. However, if you are in the health and nutrition business where this is used to support and enhance your brand, then by all means, go for it. My posts on my personal feeds are about personal as well as professional interests and I mix the two now. No point in overthinking what is professional and what is personal anymore – things are moving too quickly to be faffing about unnecessarily. In the end, if your brand has direction and goals, those who get you will get you and those who don't are merely friends in waiting.

Tagging

Many people who unwittingly tag you might not necessarily be doing so according to your own 'brand guidelines'. In order to get it right, you could for instance have privacy settings that will allow only stuff you approve to show on your timeline. You can send a private message to them not to tag you unless you are happy with it. Please, please, please, avoid calling people out or sending negative stuff about what people have done to you online. We all have some bad stuff happen to us, but do we have to let the whole world know about them? I tell you if I share what my downs have been on social media, you will weep for me. My strategy on everything I do is to encourage, inspire and motivate and I don't have to do it through negativity – there is enough of that out there without me adding to it. I want to make people feel happy and warm inside. I might even have a little joke at my own expense – it makes people feel good to know that too. Gut-wrenching stuff should be minimal rather than every day.

The case for Niche Branding

Niche branding is very much about providing specialist products and services for a select group of people to consume. Imagine that you have a PhD in your field of expertise and you present yourself to a group of other people who are interested in what you have studied and are known for. That's serving a niche with your specialist brand offering. People get to know you for a being a specialist in your field and when your name comes up, they remember that Minerva knows everything about _____, and delivers it to a specific group of people such as _____. Her rates are real value for money because she goes over and above what is required in order to make her clients happy. I know many would say niching is a dangerous game because you have to put all your eggs in one basket. But that shouldn't really be so. We often have more than one area of expertise we just choose to focus on one at a time. Here are some of the benefits that may help make the case for developing a niche around your offering:

◊ You are the go-to-girl

◊ Able to do more with limited budget

◊ Messaging is more focused

◊ Referrals are more qualified

◊ Easier to measure results

◊ Can add on services as needed

◊ Harder to replicate by competitors

Be flexible with your niche

Flexibility is key, however because as markets move and things change, your messaging and targets may also change and this is where you have to monitor your offering and target market very carefully. This will enable you to serve them better in the longer term. They will often tell you what their needs are and what else they would like. I'm assuming that at this stage in the game, you will have a good relationship with them that makes it something special and if you have a good feedback system, you will know what they really, really want. You will know where their pain points are. You will know how to provide the panacea as well as the ability to augment what they need in order to be satisfied.

Your own Personal Branding Plan

It's all well and good having the lofty ideas that will make the Brand-YOU stand out amongst your peers. Bravo! That's the first step. What are you going to do about it to make it a reality? That's the planning bit followed up with some good old gusto, peppered with focus and a little bit of bravado. It's about making it smart for you, personalised so no one can own it but you. As I've often said, only you can do you, flawlessly. So let's look at some of the things you might decide to implement and wrap up the perfect present in the best way possible to present to those who may wish to have a piece of the sparkling gem that is you. We need to have it packaged and well presented.

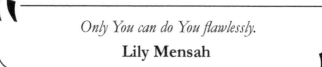

Only You can do You flawlessly.
Lily Mensah

Branded Make-over Essentials

There are many tools we can employ for brand development which I will list here as an introduction but is far from exhaustive – the idea is to start from the ground floor with what I'm sharing with you and change it up or down as you go along – after all, you are the one who has to make these work for you in an authentic and endearing way. No point in having a name tag of a CEO if you're shy and sit in the corner. As a businesswoman, you are your own billboard for your brand. Having the right attributes for your brand involves a sustainable campaign to bring the brand alive.

Business goals and your personal branding plan

There may be times where just having the odd objective for your business alone will just not bring in the changes. That is when the value of your brand can do more than just throwing money at your business goals. You have to put some skin in the game and that skin is YOU. Let's look at a couple of business goals where only a massive infusion of Brand-YOU will do the trick.

Directing the Brand-YOU

On the next page is part of an example template (download it at www.lilymensah.com/resources)that you could use to implement your brand promise and its perceived value. This will give your brand direction so you are not blindsided by trivia that doesn't add to the plan to propel you forward in a systematic and consistent way. It makes your brand message very clear. What often happens is that if you do not have

YOUR PERSONAL BRANDING PLAN					
Ultimate Goal	To be recognised as a leading voice in tax matters for female entrepreneurs, globally				
Item	Outcome	When/ how often	By whom	Budget/ time	Action/ notes
OFFLINE					
Stationery					
Logo					
Biz cards					
Office branding					
ONLINE					
Biz website					
Social media					
Blogs					
QR Code					
Email sig.					
Avatar					
IN PERSON					
Wardrobe					
videos					
Book					
Speaking					
Mentoring					
Charity					

Create your own from scratch or download the complete template at www.lilymensah.com/resources which you can then alter to suit your business.

a good plan that resonates with you and those you wish to influence, all manner of unintended activities will replace what could lead you to the holy grail of brand heaven and the outcome therefore is watered down and brand confusion becomes the norm.

Evangelists for your brand

As Naomi Klein mentioned in her book *No Logo*, she describes the brand as the spiritual home for your business and if your brand is your spiritual home, then every brand must indeed have brand evangelists who will speak eloquently and favourably on behalf of the Brand-YOU. Your job, however, is to equip them with the right messages. They come in different guises such as ambassadors, enthusiasts, influencers etcetera, but their main work is to shout out to the world how wonderful you are. Every brand needs evangelists and this for me is the true meaning of brand development. Evangelists are not paid, they just do on your behalf and you cannot really buy them – a few brands do but if you can, avoid paying those who love your brand. At every opportunity, if they are around and your name comes up, they automatically have something positive to say about you. In fact, if your name doesn't come up and there is an opportunity for your services, they will put your name forward because they believe in you and what you have to deliver.

Who in your network do you think are your evangelists? Is it time to evaluate and show them some love? In supporting you, they have your back and you must show that you have theirs. It's all about a zero-sum game where everyone wins. If I am to evangelise about your brand, I definitely need to know what it stands for and how that connects with my beliefs and values. Branding is such an emotive subject, and as much as we cannot feel it in our hands and touch it, we smell it, sense it, hear it and have a relationship with it. It's a sensory thing. Let your evangelists know that you are grateful for such support. Find ways to reach out to them often. I know we are all extremely busy but your evangelists are diamonds and will deliver more than you can ever imagine. Decipher who they are, where they are and develop a message that is consistent, congruent and constant that resonates with them in all that you do. Package it and share that message with them. They will in turn shout from the roof-tops about how wonderful you are because they know which words to use for you at the right time and place.

Measuring your brand effort

We can't just be promoting and developing tools and strategies without taking in how effective all that work is. There will be times when you make a massive effort in building brand enhancing activities but find that nothing is happening. Fear not, branding as not a one-time effort. We are in for the long haul – step by step and mile by mile, we will get there. And because we know what the destination is, we can tell if we have reached that place or whether we may have to make a detour in order to get to the desired destination.

Speaking to improve visibility

For instance, you might have decided that speaking is the thing that your brand needs but the mere thought of it makes you want to hide under the duvet and cover your head. You see, speaking takes time, practice, and a long-term strategy. My speaking career started at Toastmasters[7] in London then carried on in Orlando. Did I enjoy it? Yes. Did I make lifelong friends? Absolutely and of course, I picked up some of my best tips there. Today though, my speaking is less rigid, and perhaps as good as Toastmasters is, the style and way it's done doesn't suit the person I have become. They do take it very seriously and I like to have a bit of fun and bringing the real me to the table, warts and all. Sometimes, I'm not sure if I will ever fit into any speaking club – what I will say is that I try and take the best of each set of training and add my own quirky ways to it, and so can you.

In measuring whether your efforts are working or not, it pays to use yourself as your own yardstick. Learning tips and tricks from experienced and established people and organisations should only be a starting point. In order for you to stand out and be recognised as an authority in your field, you need to be you, not emulate someone who has done something similar. No - be you, quirks and all.

One thing I know for certain is I'm not a fan of the hand-held microphone. Don't ask me why, I hate the damn thing. I think, for me, it gives the idea of a preacher and I'm there to share, teach and often learn – not to preach. And I want to use both my hands and arms and whole body to express a point or two. Give me a lapel mic any day. Don't be afraid to treat yourself to one that you can carry with you whenever you are asked to speak because some organisers tend to only supply the hand-held ones. Even after you've requested a lapel mic; they forget or cannot find one so easily and don't tell you until you get to the venue. It's happened to me a lot so don't take it personally.

Workshops are also an option if you want to cut your teeth on the 'standing in front of people' thing before going full frontal to the stage as a speaker. I remember my first workshop as a knowledge manager at Andersen, teaching techies how to harness and manage the tacit knowledge we as a company were acquiring at an alarmingly fast rate and things were changing. It was 1999 and the lead up to Y2K and if you were around then, you will remember the messages were all about things changing and having to know everything. I was petrified to say the least because these were really bright people who knew their stuff and I was to help them manage it and share it appropriately. What did I know about pair programming and data-mining? Zilch. What I didn't realise was that I didn't need to know any of that. I just needed to be aware that I was helping the gurus do what they do best and then showing them how to share their expertise to maximise the company's knowledge arsenal and to scale it appropriately. Thankfully, a couple of sheroes, Jess Magnusson and Gem Patel came to my aid. They had done something similar for their teams in Finance and Operations and they coached me on how to get my materials right, how to stand with authority and show that I knew my stuff. It wasn't that I didn't know my stuff – it was about coming across as such. Most of us know our stuff but tend to have this sense of fear that we will either fluff our lines or perhaps the presentation might not go according to plan.

Top Tip

In a presentation, the audience will never know what you intended to say so if you forget to say something, it's OK. Only you will know what you meant to say, so don't beat yourself up about it.

If you have prepared well, it will go according to how it should be. Great, because you are in control, not the audience, not the host, but you. You will bring you into the room ready to share your knowledge so that your audience will be empowered to do more than they did before you shared your know-how. It's never about you, though – it is about them and what they take away.

I've had a couple of engagements where technical challenges have meant that there was no equipment to speak of. Imagine that! On each occasion I've said to myself that because I had prepared in advance and spent some time thinking and crafting my slides for each audience it would have been a shame not to share my knowledge and expertise just because of technology. I refuse to let technology beat me. What did people do without speakers, slides and microphones? They spoke from the heart and projected their voices, so that's what Ms Lily is damn well going to do. Because I had done my homework, I was able to do the presentations without the support of my accoutrements and guess what, no one died. Certainly not me and I lived to tell my story. The show must always go on.

So if speaking is one of your brand enhancing goals, you are in good company. Let me share a couple of tips with you that I gave someone recently who asked me what my advice was for aspiring speakers.

◊ Have some sexy, but very comfortable underwear on or spanks to avoid the jiggles if you walk on stage;

◊ Put on your Sunday best, because if you feel good, you will walk and talk with confidence;

◊ Speak to members of the audience in advance, if you are able to, so you can make at least one friend before you go on stage;

◊ Black is never a good colour if the spotlight is on you – brighter colours are better;

◊ Shoes should be a couple of inches high as they help with your posture and gait;

◊ Go to the bathroom before the speech and give yourself a massive kiss in the mirror and say to yourself "Damn – I'm gorgeous!" Do you know what that does? It checks that you are looking good and there's no lunchtime spinach lurking around in your front teeth.

If you've done a few speaking gigs, would you say you are seen as an authority in your field or were you not shouting about it? That is the acid test. If the host is good, they should promote your imminent speech well in advance and to follow-up with offers for your products, especially if it is a gig that is not paid for. If a host asks you to pay to speak, I would be very dubious about it. Speaking is a big deal and the number of hours you prepare to do an 18 minute (TED[8] Rules) speech are often in double figures and then some. Do not allow your brand to be dictated to by those who wish to use you because you are not famous yet – by all means, speak for free if you have to but don't pay to speak. This is my personal opinion but you or others might disagree and that is always their prerogative and I will always respect that.

Video creates more visibility. FACT

About 18 months ago, I was about to do my first video because that was what I had told the whole world and his wife I was going to do before the year was over. It was my number one goal and as you know if you share a goal with others, you are 50% there. So that's what I did. Then, I asked my sheroes to be my accountability partners and boy, did they hound me. In a good way though, and for that I'm grateful. I spoke to a great friend Julian about how on earth I was going to make this a reality and miraculously, he sent me or perhaps through him, God sent me this very patient and knowledgeable all-rounder in front and behind the camera kind of person. Dawn is an actress and film-maker with awards to her name. Her gift to me was making me feel comfortable and less self-conscious. Getting me to forget there was even a camera in my face – you see I would freeze at the mere fact that there was a camera in the room let alone one close to my face. So I wrote the script and everything then D-day came. I promise you, I was close to cancelling that morning but something told me that I would first of all piss Julian off for not showing and I would never find another director with such passion for what she did. So off I went for the shoot, and the rest is history. You will find the clips on my YouTube page www.youtube.com/watch?v=gAuLpYkgtCU.

What came out of this very video for me? People I had met online could hear and see me speak for the first time. "Gosh, is that you, Lily?" one message said. My name, my face and the things that I would wear often suggested that some saw me differently and until they heard me speak couldn't quite figure me out. I was approached by an acquaintance directly after that video to say it was lovely to hear me speak and actually a lovely surprise. In 2016 I've taken it to another level by doing some of my how-to tips on Instagram starting with A-Z of personal branding. I often use props such as hats to disguise the fact that I'm still petrified of the camera. What Instagram has given me is that 1-minute thing to get my message across, punchy, quick and I'm outta there. No hanging about for fluffed lines. My question to you is how do you come across and can video help you look better online? I think so – my advice is to keep it short and simple.

You could find a topic of choice to speak about such as A-Z of your brand promise. You will be amazed how quickly this will build your confidence and your following as the go-to person in your field. The trick is as women, we have to find our best sides – I think my best side is my right but that's the side that I keep getting spots if I have too much chocolate or nuts so it's really a matter of hiding the spot on 'filming-day'.

Here are some tips on getting the video right:

◊ **Wardrobe, hair and make-up** - Your clothes speak volumes on your behalf, long before you've even opened your mouth. Let your clothes therefore say it loud and clear that you are in charge of this message and what you have to say is very, very important. Dress to impress even if you are sitting in your home office shuffling paper for the VAT man. My recommendation is to keep an open neck and jewellery should also be kept to a minimum because we don't want the jewellery to take over the message we have to impart.

◊ **Hair – our crowning glory** – We touched on hair earlier too and all I can say is that your hair is no less important in the image stakes. If you are not having a good hair day, then girlfriend, get yourself a gorgeous hat. You could use a wig if you like, but would that be your everyday? Hats are more forgiving in my book because having a wig in a video and then having to meet the video watchers in person might create a visual problem. My take on being your flawless self in a video is trying not to be a different person in a video than you would be in person and hair is one thing that we women have to grapple with daily.

◊ **Face-to-face** – Your face should be made up but not too much of course. We are still aiming for the effortless chic look. I know some would say come as you are because that is your authentic self. No. I disagree. Making an effort to present yourself to the world shows. The stuff online is there Forever! And forever means that even if you delete it, someone else might have captured it before you got a chance to delete it. So all I ask is that you get your groove on before you put your face on video. Lip colour should always be more matte than gloss – say shimmery. Glossy lips, same as jewellery, call too much attention to themselves, and tend to distract from what you have to say. Remember that your lips carry the words that you say, therefore, that's where people look more than anywhere else.

◊ **Lights, camera action!** – Lighting is one of my number one props because with the correct lighting you come across brighter, happier and more engaging. Your energy is positive too. I'm sure there are energy therapists out there who will agree with me on this. Why do you think in the movies, they go 'Lights, Camera, Action'? I've often found that I do my best videos in natural lighting so most of mine are outdoors. When the weather is chillier, one may have no choice but to stay indoors in order to shoot a video and even when we do video calls, my best advice is to have extra lighting to brighten you and your attendees' experiences.

I had a chat with a lovely, outgoing woman who is quite well-known in the legal field and we spoke about *Facebook Live* and some of the challenges there about people presenting themselves and she said, '*Yes, there's facebook live, there's authenticity and then there's shit*'. I would have chosen slightly different words but I couldn't help agreeing with her. Why is it that so many big organisations hire make-up artists and other people behind the camera with scripts etc., to shoot something decent and we think we can just turn up in our pyjamas with curlers in our hair to pontificate to the masses? Remember your reputation carries on long after you've left the building. So, please take some time to present yourself to your audience, continually. It's more professional and very endearing.

Uplighters with extra options for when on video and or when you are just working by your very own self will see you sparkle rather than be in the dark when people want to see the Brand-YOU! Yes, lights all the way – the more the better, honey!

Health and Wellness Manifesto

We cannot go through our lives without topping up with goodness otherwise we will run out of gas. You being your own brand means getting some rest, eating well and making sure that you are in good shape. As women, we tend to keep going and saying yes to anyone and anything, and stopping to take stock is not often on the cards. As much as I know I have to be mindful of this flaw, I also know that I'm no expert in this field and that's why I've enlisted the help of one of my sheroes, Rachel McGuinness of Wake up with Zest to give us the ins and outs of what to do to keep the brand sparkling from a human, health and wellbeing perspective.

Rachel McGuinness - Healthy Tips

To look amazing, feel incredible, have loads of energy and preserve that precious sparkle of yours, you have to look after number one – yes, that's you! I like to think of health falling into four different categories or, as I like to call them, my four pillars of vitality. They are: sleep well, eat smart, move more and chill out. They are so inter-linked; you can't have one without the other as they are all important. For example, if you don't sleep properly it affects the way you eat as you're probably going to be reaching out for the carbs to give you an instant energy fix, then you're not going to have any energy or motivation to do any exercise, which means you may not relax because you keep thinking about all the things you should be doing, but you can't because you're too tired and then of course you get irritable and stressed with everyone, which then feeds into another bad night's sleep. Or you are stressed about work, you comfort eat and if you're stressed you may not sleep properly, no energy equals no exercise – you get my drift? You feel like you're on a perpetual merry-go-round that won't stop or a downward spiral that you can't seem to break out of.

Back in the year 2000, I was the complete antithesis of what I am now – completely un-zesty! In those days I smoked like a chimney, drank like a fish, attacked food like a Pacman, was a professional couch potato and was on my way to burn out and some serious health problems if I didn't start to look after myself. Can you believe I actually spent 22 years on diets that never worked? It left me at a size 18 instead of the size 10 which I always aspired to be. It was only a chance sighting of my reflection in a mirror while on a business trip to Barcelona that motivated me to start looking after number one. So what were my secrets to getting my sparkle and finding my inner diamond?

IT'S ALL ABOUT MIND-SET
Before we dive into the four pillars, one thing you must do to get the results you want is to change your attitude around being healthy. Healthy isn't all about hard graft, deprivation, torturing yourself and will-power; it is all about mind-set. It is all about embracing a healthier

lifestyle, if you're going to look after you, you can no longer maintain your self-destructive unhealthy habits. So being healthy is all about mind-set change around living a healthier lifestyle.

SLEEP WELL

The first thing is to focus on your sleep. Believe me, you need your beauty sleep to maintain your sparkle, help that inner diamond shine on through and give you that much needed va-va-voom. If you want to be smarter, slimmer, sexier and stronger – get more sleep! Get into a bedtime routine, go to bed at more or less the same time every night (yes even at weekends). Cut your alcohol and caffeine consumption to avoid nocturnal trips to the loo as they are both diuretics. Unweld yourself from your tech about an hour to an hour and half before bedtime. Screens on phones and tablets emit blue light which wakes you up when you should be nice and sleepy and can therefore disrupt your sleep; also try to keep your phone out of the bedroom. Keep your bedroom like a cave; cool, dark and well-ventilated. The ideal temperature for sleeping is around 16 degrees centigrade.

EAT SMART

What you eat will definitely affect your sparkle. I am a great believer in eating a low carb diet which is high in protein and healthy fats to either lose weight or maintain a healthy one. No, before you ask, I am not an advocate of the Atkins Diet! When I use the word diet I mean it in the food that we eat not as a way to lose weight. Oh, and if you want to lose weight DON'T DIET! Remember I spent 22 years on diets that never worked! If you want to lose weight, eat healthily and watch your portion sizes. The easy way to work out your portion sizes is to use your hands. The size of your protein should be size of the palm of your hand without the fingers, veg or salad should be size of one and a half fists and your carb (potato, pasta, rice) should be half a fist or none at all. Your fruit should be the size of your fist which is the size of an apple or orange, use the same volume for smaller fruits or berries.

Eat any of the protein from the following healthy list; meat, fish, poultry, seafood, eggs, seeds, nuts, dairy and non-dairy which could be sheep, goat or plant based. Eat no more than three pieces of fruit per day to minimise your sugar intake and leave five hour gaps between meals to allow your body to fat burn. If you need to snack, snack on something protein based like a little bit of cheese or a few nuts. Always eat three meals a day; you can't fire on all cylinders if you skip breakfast.

My top tip for eating smart is to plan your menus for the week and get organised to make sure you've always got healthy food in your cupboard, fridge and freezer, then you're not on auto dial to the local takeaway because you've run out of food!

MOVE MORE

Exercise will give you added sparkle too. Humans aren't designed to sit behind a desk all day every day, we are designed to move three to five miles a day, which is around 10,000 steps. I used to be allergic to exercise after being regularly humiliated at games in school, however when I decided to get healthy and changed my mind-set, I learned to love it, because I'm doing what I enjoy, at my own pace and getting great results and to me that's what counts. The great news is that you don't have to spend hours in the gym flogging yourself to death on a treadmill or going to classes where everyone ignores each other, and guess what you can get fit and toned without leaving your home. I believe in doing the three S's:

- Strength
- Sweat
- Stretch.

Let's look at each of them in more detail.

Strength – I love High Intensity Interval Training (HIIT), it sounds scary, but don't be put off by the name. All it is, is short bursts of activity such as 20 to 40 seconds with a 10 second rest which gets repeated generally for four minutes. What is even better, you can get great results in three to four 10 to 15 minute workouts per week. All you have to do to get your hands on these gems is Google 'free HIIT workouts' and you can pick and choose what you like and don't like. All you need is a yoga mat or a set of dumb bells, as most of the workouts are based on using your own body weight.

Sweat – If you do HIIT, I can guarantee you will sweat as well; they are a 'get a lot of bang for your buck' workouts. However, if you want to run, swim, play tennis, football, netball, hockey etc then do it, but my advice is to put some HIIT workouts in too.

Stretch – Stretching is so good for you and very important, especially if you've been sitting on your tush all day long at a desk or behind the wheel of a car, then spend the evening slumped on the sofa watching the latest Netflix box set. Sitting for long periods of time can lead to problems with posture and back pain. Yoga and or Pilates or even just gentle stretching are the best ways to get your body back into realignment and prevent aches, pains and strains.

CHILL OUT

The final sparkly pillar is to make sure you take time out for you to relax, recharge and re-energise. This is so important, as we all lead very busy lives, if you don't do this, it could be affecting your stress levels and your ability to sleep well. Chilling out is about just being, being in the moment and enjoying the present. Take the opportunity to lose yourself in a good book, go for a walk or exercise some self-care and treat yourself to a massage or a beauty treatment, or even do a face mask or manicure at home.

Meditation is also a fantastic way of helping you de-stress and clear your head, and you can reap the many benefits in as little as 10 minutes. If the thought of sitting silently for 10 minutes fills you with fear, go online and search for guided meditations.

Giving yourself permission to take time out for you is so important whether you decide to spend it by yourself or with others. If you are with others, make sure you spend time with people who make you happy and not the energy vampires or mood hoovers!

I hope my four pillars give you lots of inner and outer sparkle and of course zestiness!

Rachel McGuinness – Wake Up With Zest

In fairness – I, Lily, have been guilty too of not taking care of me as well as I could have done. What then happened was that I felt less than perfect almost to the point of having huge challenges with the slightest thing that didn't sit right with me. I was saying yes, too often, to the wrong people who just took and when I couldn't give any more, they suddenly wondered, oh, what happened here? I thought everything was cool.

Once I moved back to being me and taking my time to do me with complete self-love, I got my balance and my mojo back. It takes something to shift for you to realise that you might be saying yes for the wrong reasons, and unless we take stock, we will be on someone else's treadmill where the reading from the workout is not linked to your overall results but theirs. Some may see self-love as selfish, that's their prerogative – I see it as one of the most beneficial things you can do for you and those around you. If you feel good, you do good and everyone benefits. If on the other hand you are rushed off your feet, thinking and doing all the time, you will not be a nice person to hang around with and the end result will be loss of health, friends, loved ones and much more.

CHAPTER 10

A Sparkling Brand that's Uniquely You

> *Life's not worth a dime until you can shout that I am, what I am!*
> **Gloria Gaynor**

In the preceding chapters, we've talked about your quirks, creating your own personal diamonds around your goals, your expertise, your competition, wardrobe and online profiles amongst other things. I have thoroughly enjoyed sharing what I know with you in the hope that you will in turn share with other business women who are on the rise, about to change or upscale in direction. I hope the gems from my contributors and sheroes, Helen, Mavis, Stella and Rachel added more sparkle to the brand building exercises.

We are all work in progress and some of the weird and wonderful things that have happened to me have made me who I am today. I have met some amazing women in my life who have been so generous with their knowledge and expertise and I hope I've been able to reciprocate when I could. Our Quirks are very much our own. They cannot be replicated in their entirety. We may have the same skills, described as being the same in a certain category but the way we deliver our services with our brands will almost always differ. Even twins differ in their approach to things.

There is a song that I equate to the concept of personal branding which has been rejigged many a time by various artistes. I believe the original is by Johnny Mercer and the Pied Pipers back in the 1940s though my favourite rendition is by the Goddess of Soul, Aretha Franklin and it goes something like this:

> # You've got to
> ## Ac-Cent-Tchu-Ate the positive;
> ## Eliminate the negative;
> ## Latch on to the affirmative;
> ## But don't mess with Mister in between

So what exactly does that mean for Brand-YOU?

Ac-Cent-Tchu-Ate the positive

Finding the things that you are good at, that make your heart sing, and telling the world about them would be great for your brand. It's that gift, that God-given talent that only you can call your own because of the way YOU deliver it. Accentuate all the positive elements of your brand and tell the world about it. That's personal branding 101. You have to be comfortable about bragging a little, or a lot, depending on where you are, of course. But tell it you must. Go tell it on the mountain, over the hills and everywhere as one of my favourite hymns goes. You have to tell it, over and over again to the right people and eventually, those who want to and need to hear your message will get it. Some will get it very quickly; others might take a little time to latch on which is OK too.

Eliminate the negative

We all have something we are absolutely atrocious at or things we need to get rid of be it a skill, a weight issue, (I'm with you on that if that's you) or just plain time leeches. It's important to know what they are and if you can do something about it, do so and if you cannot do anything about it, learn to live with it in a way that doesn't put a dimmer on your sparkle. It might even be energy vampires. If they see a weakness, the leeches will pounce. Be mindful and stay away from negativity as they don't add but take away from the diamond in the making.

Latch on to the affirmative

Yes, yes, yessss! What I mean by this is that we must constantly seek the things that affirm our unique promise in the areas where we feel our best selves. It's important to look within the places and the people that welcome us and help us to sparkle. For example, those networks online and offline that we feel comfortable in whilst looking at other opportunities. Those places and people that prompt us to try harder, knowing full well that if we fall, they will pull out the sheets to catch us. For instance, I'm still a massive fan of LinkedIn despite its masculine and high-brow appearance. I've made a great career out of being different so I sit comfortably there but my observation is that, we as female entrepreneurs are not vocal there at all. Why is that? I'm still working on that bit of research. That said, Facebook is the place where most of us hang out so I'm learning to hang out there professionally too. As for Twitter, that's an untapped place for business owners but we are not using it that well and I often have to ask why and I'm told it's just too limiting. If you don't have anything to say in 140 words put a picture and add your caption. Easy! Now I have a new found love called Instagram – just pictures and one-minute videos. For me that is pure Heaven. You see I'm not a big fan of long-winded videos as I really do not have time to (1) to listen and (2) to decipher which bits I'm to find useful. So if I listen to my own advice, that means I work quietly in the background until I have something useful to say. In my view people will listen more because you are not going on and on pontificating about this and that that doesn't have value.

Find what works for you and stick with it, tweak occasionally, if you have to. It's about perceived value not creating content because you have to do X number of videos or articles a month.

But don't mess with Mister in-between

Wishy-washy is not brand-friendly. Period. You are either one thing or you are not. When we sit in between we can create confusion about what makes us unique, what our QUIRKs are and what could potentially make us sparkle. There will always be those who say play safe. Safe is great in the right setting. Don't get me wrong. If you have a valid reason for playing safe, I don't want to be the one to get your brand in trouble by saying go and do what is brand-limiting. However, sitting on the fence and not voicing your opinion or showing some backbone will eventually limit your brand-enhancing sparkle. In other words, *"you shy, you die"*, so said by another personal branding powerhouse, John Antonios. It's a phrase I use quite often especially when I'm coaching someone who is being tentative about stepping out because being shy might be crippling their style and holding back their unique promise.

Personal branding has that one unintentional consequence which is to give you confidence to step out. Why? Because you have all your ducks in a row and you know you can and will accentuate the positive. You are absolutely certain with what you are good at, the best cut for your wardrobe, who your ideal clients are and the message that you would have crafted to sell yourself without trying too much. A consequence that is positive, too.

SUMMARY

I'm absolutely certain that each and every one of us has that unique brilliance that will dazzle even the most hardened critics of the personal branding movement. Just like diamonds in the rough, we are often under several tons of earth and our jobs involve doing all we can to bring our brand promise to the fore and then find ways to make that promise sparkle. We are able to withstand extreme pressure without buckling, we take so much heat and smile through some dark moments with complete aplomb. We compete on our own terms in order to become brands worthy of note. We can even re-write the rulebook, such as networking differently from the way men do.

How we craft our messages and delivery around our marketing and promotional messages must be authentic and engaging. Perception is often all that people have and that then becomes others reality of our brands. Having that consistency and constancy means we will be known for something or just a handful of things. If we are all things to all women, pun intended, few will beat down our doors in order to buy into that perceived value. Conversely, if we have a finely crafted message or series of messages that point to the same thing, then we have a winning formula that people will remember and be able to refer to if needs be.

Branding is a cycle that doesn't stop once you have gone through a series of processes. Brands need refreshing, things change, opportunities come and go and industries may have a shift. We have to make that shift too if we are to be more relevant in the areas that we have chosen to serve. We cannot do a onetime branding thing and leave it there to sell on our behalf while we sleep. We must continually find ways to keep our brands sparkling and where better than to ask your current network for feedback to help tweak any areas that need improvement. We may not need to do a complete rebrand by going through the research, review, reveal and refine process again, but we may well have to find a new way of adding a fifth 'R', Relevance, to the brand enhancing process.

By using all our God-given talents to be all that we can be means that like diamonds, which are not called the transparent stone for nothing, we are also more valuable the more authentic we are. As much as some of the processes today may have changed in making diamonds, the cutting remains in the hands of the master cutter. We are the master-cutters of our brand promise. The professionalism, the cut, and presentation will determine our ultimate value.

I hope you have found some nuggets in this book and my wish for you is nothing but mega success and a sparkling brand that is uniquely you!

MAY EVERYTHING YOU WISH FOR, BE THE LEAST THAT YOU RECEIVE.

ACKNOWLEDGEMENTS

I'd like to acknowledge the following without whom this book would never have seen the light of day. Their contributions, support, gentle nudging, counsel and downright "just get on with it, will you" type of looks. I'm so grateful, you didn't walk ahead of me, you didn't walk behind me, you walked by my side and occasionally held my hand when I was ready to throw in the towel.

Massive thanks to Penny Power OBE, for saying yes to penning a brilliant foreword; Helen Walbey, Mavis Amankwah, Stella Fehmi and Rachel McGuinness for your generous contributions to Work Your Quirks; Sarah Houldcroft for showing me the infinite possibilities available to me as an author and publisher; Amanda Quartey for her creativity in illustrating my ideas so well, yet punctuated with her own unique style. Oyiwaladon to Auntie Margaret Dubner for your teachings, encouragement and entrepreneurial savvy and all the women who have in their own way helped me with either kind words, encouraging nods, tips or tricks and also those who have challenged me. Too many to name here – I thank you ALL!

And finally to my "TOWGA" who has stood by my side no matter what – we've had teary moments, laughed until we couldn't hold our waters any longer and also prayed together when that was all that would save our sorry behinds. I wouldn't have you any other way.

ABOUT THE AUTHOR

Lily Naadu Mensah

Multi Award-winning business & brand strategist

Lily Mensah's career in branding and client facing communication spans over 20 years, the last 15 of which have taken her as far as Accra, London and the Space Coast in Florida. She's the Managing Director and Brand Ambassador of Lyncs Media, www.lyncsmedia.com

My job is to see your personal brand sparkle!

After long stints working with Lloyds of London and Arthur Andersen, she decided to use her entrepreneurial flair to invigorate socially conscious individuals and organisations into purposefully creating brand awareness responsibly. She quickly realised that if she was ever going to make her clients successful, she needed to go beyond logos and widgets and get to the nitty-gritty of why people buy. She now specialises in personal branding for entrepreneurs and professionals to co-create *powerful, viable* and *visible* results. Whether its wardrobe consulting, online profiles or marketing materials, Lily can be counted on to make your brand sparkle!

Her experience with famous and notorious brands is invaluable in helping professionals who might be in a bit of a quandary as to how their values can successfully influence their business and career direction.

She has worked in the United Kingdom, with Baroness Howells of St David's and Lord Soley of Hammersmith; made presentations to diverse audiences such as NASA (Florida) and the London Development Agency; is a trained mentor for young adults and a member of the Institute of Management Consultancy.

A Reach certified brand strategist and speaker, Lily also has her own radio show called Tea-With-Lily where she interviews the great and the good on issues for professional and personal growth.

Lily received an award of recognition from the Mayor of Bromley in the UK, for her outstanding contribution towards making Bromley, one of the most successful local business communities. Her most recent nod was from GAB (Gathering of Africa's Best) Awards, in recognition for her Marketing Consultancy Services.

CONTACT THE AUTHOR

You can contact Lily Naadu Mensah in the following ways:

Skype: Brand-U

Twitter: ladymensah

www.lyncsmedia.com

http://about.me/lilymensah

www.blogtalkradio.com/ladymensah

lily@lilymensah.com

REFERENCES & RESOURCES

References

(1) Page 12 www.baunat.com/en/faq/are-diamonds-rare

(2) Page 12 www.time.com/money/3896219/internet-users-worldwide/

(3) Page 84 Raconteur: www.raconteur.net/the-beauty-economy-2015

(4) Page 88 Psychologies magazine: www.psychologies.co.uk/body/the-power-of-red-lipstick.html

(5) Page 112 www.linkedin.com/pulse/2016-linkedin-stats-you-should-know-updated-katy-elle-blake?published=t

(6) Page 125 Pew Research: http://www.pewresearch.org/

(7) Page 132 www.toastmasters.org

(8) Page 136 www.ted.com

Downloads

Page 60 Download: Design & creative brief www.lilymensah.com/resources

Page 81 Download: Colour wheel www.lilymensah.com/resources

Page 130 Download: Personal Branding Plan www.lilymensah.com/resources

Resources

Page 24 360Reach Personal Branding Survey: www.reachcc.com/360v5register

Page 25 SurveyMonkey: www.surveymonkey.com/

Page 36 VIA institute: www.viacharacter.org/www/Character-Strengths-Survey

Page 37 Helen Walbey: MD of Recycle Scooters and National Policy Chair for Health and Diversity at Federation of Small Businesses, www.fsb.org.uk

Page 54 Mavis Amankwah: www.mavisamankwah.com

Page 86 www.elizabetharden.co.uk/facial-services.list

Page 87 www.marieclaire.com/beauty/news/a7043/makeup-affects-career-study/

Page 99 QR Generator: www.the-qrcode-generator.com

Page 103 Stella Fehmi: www.theathenanetwork.co.uk/StellaFehmi/stella-fehmi-regional-director-city-and-west-essex/

Page 122 BeBee: www.bebee.com

Page 122 Brandyourself: www.Brandyourself.com

Page 122 AboutMe: www.about.me

Page 132 Toastmasters: www.toastmasters.org

Page 137 My video: YouTube page www.youtube.com/watch?v=gAuLpYkgtCU

Page 140 Rachel McGuinness: www.wakeupwithzest.com